JAMIE OLIVER

5 INGREDIENTS MEDITERRANEAN

Food photography DAVID LOFTUS

Design JAMES VERITY

MICHAEL JOSEPH

PENGUIN
Est. 1935

LLOYD HAYES

1983 — 2023

This year one of our much-loved graduates from the Fifteen training programme was taken from us far too early.

The Fifteen crew and I are devastated by his passing. When I first met Lloyd, he was a bubbly, strapping lad, with a formidable presence, and big hands that had, up until then, gotten him into a few too many scrapes. But he was determined to turn things around. And his transformation into a fine cook was powerful to us all. Quickly, those same strong hands ended up making some of the most delicate, exquisite food.

He was honest, spoke his truth and was a brilliant team player, and I wanted to support him in opening his first restaurant. But sadly, cancer had other plans. His remarkable rise from the first day I met him reaffirmed my strong belief that giving young people second chances and the time and tools to succeed is imperative for our communities to flourish.

He leaves behind his wonderful wife Natasha and two gorgeous kids, Ashton and Aalayah, who will always be a big part of our Fifteen family.

Rest in peace, brother.

CONTENTS

DELICIOUS
BIG-FLAVOUR FOOD

This book was somewhat unplanned. I didn't think I'd ever write another *5 Ingredients*, but I've lost count of the number of times I've been asked to do so, especially by my wife, Jools. She told me to stop thinking about anything else: 'It's where people are at, when our lives are so incredibly busy – it's the book all the parents at school talk about.'

Now I've never really been one to revisit old territory and repeat a scenario, but it's a sign of the times. People cook very differently today in comparison to 50 or even 25 years ago when I first started – there's just so much more we have to fit into our busy lives, and the way tech has grown around us, it has both given and taken time away. Plus, it's human nature to find the most efficient way to gain back time, but fill it with something else! And so, with this in mind, I've written you another *5 Ingredients* cookbook with the added va-va-voom of basing it on my lifelong experiences travelling around the Mediterranean – one of the most loved and respected diets in the world, where simplicity, love, passion, care and dedication to taste and big flavour are at its heart.

5 INGREDIENTS

When I write a solution-based book like this, I always have you, the reader, at the forefront of my mind, with the aim of holding your hand and guiding you to make everyday cooking super-exciting, but with minimal fuss. In a quest to keep things fresh and inspiring, the TV show that accompanies this book takes us to some incredible places around the Mediterranean, full of such diverse culture and truly extraordinary flavours. And, as you turn the pages that follow, I hope you get a real sense of the countries, cities and islands that I've been to, both recently and also throughout my travels over the last 25 years. The Med is a beautiful and diverse area, consisting of at least 22 countries (although other countries swear they are part of it), and different as they all are, they have the sea and all its wonders in common. So, I've really tried to scatter these recipes to as many parts as I can with the experiences I've had. This is just the tip of the iceberg, but I really hope you're going to love these recipes – they're a real celebration of hero Mediterranean ingredients, flavours and combinations.

A REAL CELEBRATION OF HERO MEDITERRANEAN INGREDIENTS, FLAVOURS & COMBINATIONS

Cooking delicious big-flavour food with just 5 ingredients requires you to be clever, thrifty and resourceful, and that's my job here – to diplomatically translate some of the essence of different cuisines and bring them back home, through the reality of your local supermarket, into your house, and ultimately on to your family table and into their rumbling tummies. In effect, that means using common sense with regard to what's readily available, which is why you'll find plenty of ingredient hacks and flavour bombs throughout these recipes to give you more bang for your buck.

Believe it or not, we've never cooked less than we do right now. The food industry is geared towards convenience, and with most of us leading busy lives, we understandably lap it up. So this is not just a cookbook to be trusted and useful to you, it's also one of my efforts to keep cooking alive in an accesssible and relevant way. Within the culture of food, the saying 'Use it or lose it' is true, and I think we're all better off as humans if we keep cooking, and keep connected to our ingredients and farmers, and know how to nourish ourselves with delicious meals in good times and bad. Not to mention that warm feeling we get when we cook for someone we love, knowing what's gone into it.

My main intention with these recipes is to empower you with simple, easy and delicious food, but without copious amounts of ingredients, long shopping lists or a whole load of washing-up. It's perfect for beginner cooks, but if it's anything like the last book, many advanced cooks will love it too, because regardless of their talent for cooking, they too are time-poor and juggling a thousand things just to get through the week.

I've purposefully kept the layout of the book super-clean, and the recipes as short and to the point as possible, each with a visual ingredients key, so that you can easily get cracking. This book is not one for nostalgia, it's about providing a whole rainbow of simple meal solutions and deliciousness, and getting it to your table with minimal fuss. I've done my best to do the thinking and heavy-lifting for you – I hope it helps you out, I hope you love the recipes as much as I do, and most of all, I hope it transports you to the beyond-beautiful Mediterranean, 5-ingredients style. Big Love,

Jamie
x

5 INGREDIENT PANTRY

As with all my recent books, I always presume you've got these five everyday basic ingredients. They consistently pop up in every recipe and aren't included in the five key ingredients pictured on each page. These five heroes are olive oil for cooking, extra virgin olive oil for dressing and finishing dishes, red wine vinegar as a good all-rounder when it comes to acidity and balancing marinades, sauces and dressings, and, of course, sea salt and black pepper for seasoning to perfection.

For helpful kitchen notes, turn to page 300.

SALADS

ISLAND SALAD
STICKY PEACHES, HALLOUMI WEB & PICKLED CUCUMBER

Whenever I've visited the Greek islands, I've been inspired by wonderful fresh and fruity halloumi salads, so I've had some fun here creating little webs of golden crispy halloumi that just eat so well.

SERVES 2 | **TOTAL 15 MINUTES**

1 cucumber

2 pittas

1 x 415g tin of sliced peaches in juice

120g mixed salad leaves

60g halloumi cheese

Speed-peel the cucumber lengthways into long ribbons, discarding the seedy core, and place in a bowl with a pinch of sea salt and black pepper, and 1 tablespoon each of red wine vinegar and extra virgin olive oil. Toast the pittas, then slice into strips and arrange around the edges of two plates.

Place a large non-stick frying pan on a high heat. Drain and roughly chop the peaches (reserving the juice), then place in the pan with a good splash of the reserved juice, and season with pepper. Warm through for a few minutes while you toss the salad leaves with the dressed cucumber, and plate up. Remove the peaches to a bowl, give the pan a quick wipe with a ball of kitchen paper, then use the fine side of a box grater to grate half the halloumi over the surface of the pan (like a lacy doily). Leave on the heat for 1 to 2 minutes, or until golden on one side, then tip directly over one of the plates, using a spatula to ease it away from the pan, if needed. Repeat with the remaining halloumi for the second plate. Spoon over the peaches, and tuck straight in.

ENERGY	FAT	SAT FAT	PROTEIN	CARBS	SUGARS	SALT	FIBRE
361kcal	15.2g	6g	15.9g	39.8g	12.3g	1.3g	4.1g

CHARRED OKRA SALAD
BLISTERED TOMATOES, DUKKAH, TAHINI-RIPPLED YOGHURT

You'll often find okra in Eastern Mediterranean markets, in all different sizes and colours. I really love to dry-grill it, and with the sweetness of blistered tomatoes, it makes a wonderful warm salad.

SERVES 2 | TOTAL 12 MINUTES

250g okra

250g ripe mixed-colour cherry tomatoes

4 tablespoons natural yoghurt

2 tablespoons tahini

1 heaped tablespoon dukkah, plus extra to serve

Trim any ends off the okra stalks, then place in a screaming-hot griddle pan on a high heat with the cherry tomatoes and spread out into a single layer. Cook for 10 minutes, shaking regularly – you may need to work in batches. Meanwhile, spoon the yoghurt on to a serving platter, ripple in the tahini, then season lightly with sea salt and black pepper. Once the okra and tomatoes are charred and blistered, carefully tip them into a large bowl. Scatter over the dukkah, add 2 tablespoons of extra virgin olive oil and a splash of red wine vinegar, then toss and season to perfection. Spoon over the platter, and finish with an extra pinch of dukkah and a drizzle of extra virgin olive oil, if you like.

ENERGY	FAT	SAT FAT	PROTEIN	CARBS	SUGARS	SALT	FIBRE
340kcal	26.5g	5.1g	11.2g	14.3g	10.6g	0.8g	3.9g

A REALLY FRENCH SALAD
MUSTARDY BLISTERED BEANS, GOAT'S CHEESE & WALNUTS

I wanted to challenge myself to put these classically French ingredients together in a surprising way, and so this salad was born – smoky beans, oozy cheese and a punchy mustardy dressing. Voilà!

SERVES 2 WITH LEFTOVER DRESSING | **TOTAL 18 MINUTES**

160g fine green beans

1 tablespoon Dijon mustard

100g wheel of goat's cheese, with edible rind

20g shelled unsalted walnut halves

60g lamb's lettuce

Place a large non-stick frying pan on a high heat. Trim the beans and dry fry for 10 minutes, or until nicely blistered and tender, tossing occasionally. Meanwhile, mix the mustard and 4 tablespoons each of red wine vinegar and extra virgin olive oil in a jam jar with a big pinch of sea salt and black pepper. Put the lid on and shake to emulsify (I like to make a batch and save it in the fridge for another day). Once tender, remove the beans to a large bowl with 2 tablespoons of the dressing and toss together.

Turn the heat to medium, then halve the goat's cheese across the middle and place cut side up in the pan. Crumble the walnuts in and around the pan, spooning them on to the melting cheese when they're beautifully golden and toasted. Leave for a couple of minutes – the cheese will start to melt and burst out of the sides to create crispy bits, but with an oozy and delicious middle. Turn off the heat and leave to stand for 1 minute while you toss the lamb's lettuce with the mustardy beans. Divide everything between two plates, using a fish slice to carefully transfer the melty goat's cheese on top.

ENERGY	FAT	SAT FAT	PROTEIN	CARBS	SUGARS	SALT	FIBRE
295kcal	25.7g	8.9g	10.6g	4.9g	3.7g	0.6g	3.2g

NAKED SALAD TUNISIENNE
JUICY RIPE TOMATOES, CUCUMBER, APPLE & FRESH MINT

My kids absolutely love this stripped-back version of a salad Tunisienne. Traditionally served with tuna, boiled eggs and olives, I think of it as a Tunisian-style niçoise. Amazing spooned over grilled fish.

SERVES 4 TO 6 AS A SIDE | **TOTAL 18 MINUTES**

1 small red onion

2 large ripe plum tomatoes

1 green eating apple

1 cucumber

1 bunch of mint (30g)

For me, this salad is all about taking pride in delicately dicing everyday ingredients into something really beautiful. Peel the onion, quarter and deseed the tomatoes, core the apple and trim the cucumber, then take care to very finely dice everything. Pick the baby mint leaves and reserve for garnish, then very finely chop the rest, discarding the stalks. Dress everything with 3 tablespoons of extra virgin olive oil and 2 tablespoons of red wine vinegar, then season to perfection with sea salt and black pepper and scatter over the reserved mint leaves. Great served with warm flatbreads.

ENERGY	FAT	SAT FAT	PROTEIN	CARBS	SUGARS	SALT	FIBRE
132kcal	10.3g	1.4g	1.5g	8.7g	7.6g	0g	1.9g

GRILLED ASPARAGUS
SPECIAL SALMOREJO SAUCE, PATA NEGRA & PAPRIKA

Salmorejo is a cold and creamy classic Spanish soup, which I've used as inspiration for my sauce. I've made it thicker, a bit like mayo, and it eats so well with the asparagus, Pata Negra and smoky paprika.

SERVES 4 | **TOTAL 14 MINUTES**

500g asparagus

250g mixed-colour cherry tomatoes

150g sourdough bread

100g Pata Negra or quality Spanish ham

smoked paprika, for dusting

Place a griddle pan on a high heat. Snap the woody ends off the asparagus, then add the stalks to the pan and cook until tender and bar-marked all over, turning occasionally. Meanwhile, place the tomatoes in a blender (I've used yellow and orange here, but any combination works well) with 2 tablespoons of olive oil and a pinch of sea salt and black pepper. Remove the crusts from the bread, run the bread quickly under the tap, squeeze out the water, then add to the blender. Whiz until super-smooth with 1 teaspoon of red wine vinegar, adding a splash of water to loosen, if needed. Season to perfection and divide between plates. Top with the grilled asparagus, arrange the ham nicely on top, drizzle with a little extra virgin olive oil and dust with smoked paprika, to serve.

ENERGY	FAT	SAT FAT	PROTEIN	CARBS	SUGARS	SALT	FIBRE
247kcal	10.7g	2.3g	14.4g	24.4g	5.7g	1.8g	3.7g

RUBY BULGUR SALAD
RED PEPPER DRESSING, HUNG YOGHURT & GREENS

Using bulgur in lots of different ways – in soups, stews and salads – is common all over the Med, and what I love about this is that it could be a lunch, a side with meat or fish, or part of a table of dishes.

SERVES 4 | **TOTAL 30 MINUTES**

500g natural yoghurt

300g bulgur wheat

320g seasonal greens, such as chard, kale, cabbage

1 x 460g jar of roasted red peppers

1 heaped teaspoon ground cinnamon

Line a sieve with a few pieces of kitchen paper, tip in the yoghurt, then pull up the paper and very gently apply pressure so that the liquid starts to drip through into a bowl. Leave in the fridge to drain. Meanwhile, cook the bulgur in a large pan of boiling salted water according to the packet instructions. Wash and trim the greens, as necessary, finely chopping any stalks. Place the stalks in a colander with a lid on top and place above the bulgur pan to steam. After 5 minutes, add the leaves and steam for a further 5 minutes, or until just wilted. Lay the greens out on a clean tea towel and once cool enough to handle, pile them in the centre, wrap them up and wring out really well to remove the excess liquid. Finely chop, season to taste and toss with a little extra virgin olive oil, then put aside.

Meanwhile, drain the peppers, tip them into a blender and whiz with the cinnamon and 1 tablespoon each of extra virgin olive oil and red wine vinegar. Drain the bulgur and leave to steam for 5 minutes, then tip into a serving bowl. Pour over the dressing and mix well, then season to perfection. Spoon the greens on top, dollop over the hung yoghurt and drizzle with extra virgin olive oil, if you like.

ENERGY	FAT	SAT FAT	PROTEIN	CARBS	SUGARS	SALT	FIBRE
465kcal	14.1g	4.7g	16.7g	71.2g	13.1g	1g	6.5g

CREAMY WHITE BEAN SALAD
CHARRED BROCCOLI, HERBY ONION PICKLE & BOQUERONES

Using nutritious creamy beans in contrast with charred broccoli, crunchy pickles and the tang of anchovies takes this salad to the next level – serve warm or cold, and as tapas, a light lunch or side.

SERVES 2 | **TOTAL 20 MINUTES**

½ a bunch of flat-leaf parsley (15g)

½ a red onion

200g tenderstem broccoli

1 x 400g tin of cannellini beans

8 boquerones (pickled anchovies)

Pick the parsley leaves and put aside, and finely slice the stalks. Peel and very finely chop the onion, then place in a bowl with the parsley stalks, 2 tablespoons of red wine vinegar and a pinch of sea salt and black pepper. Mix well, then leave aside to lightly pickle.

Boil the kettle. Place a large non-stick frying pan on a high heat. Trim the broccoli, slice into delicate florets and dry-fry in batches until tender and charred, removing to serving plates as you go. Dress with a little extra virgin olive oil and season to perfection with salt and pepper. Tip the beans into the pan (juices and all), add a splash of boiling kettle water, allow to simmer, thicken and get creamy, then spoon over the broccoli. Add the parsley leaves and a swig of extra virgin olive oil to the onions, toss together, then scatter all over the broccoli and beans. Halve the boquerones lengthways, drape over the top, and drizzle over a little extra virgin olive oil, if you like.

ENERGY	FAT	SAT FAT	PROTEIN	CARBS	SUGARS	SALT	FIBRE
305kcal	14.4g	2.3g	20.6g	19.4g	5.4g	1.4g	12.6g

WARM HALLOUMI SALAD
FRISÉE LETTUCE, DILL, HARISSA & CARAMELIZED PEACHES

Here I've taken hero ingredients from different parts of the Med to create this seriously interesting and very different warm salad – a sweet, sour, salty and bitter harmony, great as a main or a side.

SERVES 4 | **TOTAL 12 MINUTES**

2 ripe peaches

1 x 225g block of halloumi cheese

1 head of frisée

½ a bunch of dill (10g)

1 tablespoon rose harissa

Destone the peaches, then cut into 2cm chunks, along with the halloumi. Place in a large non-stick frying pan on a high heat with 2 tablespoons of olive oil and cook for 4 minutes, turning until the halloumi is golden all over. Meanwhile, pick the really white and yellow bits off the frisée (the darker leaves don't eat well, so discard), and pick the dill. Stir the harissa into the pan with 1 tablespoon of red wine vinegar. Remove from the heat, toss in the picked frisée and dill (or tip the leaves straight on to a platter and top with the halloumi and peaches, if you prefer more of a crunch), season to perfection (if your peaches aren't beautifully ripe, you can always balance the sweetness with a little honey) and serve.

ENERGY	FAT	SAT FAT	PROTEIN	CARBS	SUGARS	SALT	FIBRE
264kcal	20.8g	10.4g	14.3g	6.1g	5.2g	1.8g	0.3g

WATERMELON SALAD
CREAMY MOZZARELLA, CELERY, FENNEL & CHERRY TOMATOES

Incredibly simple, this vibrant Sardinian-inspired salad elevates the elegance of celery and fennel, plus in combination with sweet watermelon and mozzarella it's both refreshing and ridiculously delicious.

SERVES 4 AS A MAIN OR 6 AS A SIDE | **TOTAL 15 MINUTES**

1 head of celery

1 bulb of fennel, ideally with leafy tops

250g mixed-colour cherry tomatoes

¼ of a watermelon (800g)

2 x 125g balls of buffalo mozzarella

Strip off the outer sticks of celery (and save for another day) and pull off and reserve the pale yellow inner leaves. Trim and very finely slice the rest of the celery and place in a bowl. Reserving any leafy tops, trim and finely slice the fennel and halve or quarter the cherry tomatoes, then add to the bowl. Remove the watermelon skin, picking out any large seeds, then slice into 2cm cubes, adding to the bowl as you go. Toss everything together with a good pinch of sea salt and black pepper, and 2 tablespoons each of extra virgin olive oil and red wine vinegar. Divide between plates or arrange on a large platter and spoon over the juices. Tear over the mozzarella, season with extra pepper, and scatter over the reserved celery leaves and fennel tops (if you have any).

ENERGY	FAT	SAT FAT	PROTEIN	CARBS	SUGARS	SALT	FIBRE
197kcal	12.6g	6g	9.3g	12.6g	12.5g	0.7g	0.5g

CHARRED BRUSSELS
CREAMY DRESSING, CROUTONS & SHAVED PARMESAN

A really fun and delicious dish to make. I'm using Brussels sprouts, but you can use the same charring principle for any Mediterranean brassicas, like sprouting broccoli, kale, cauliflower and romanesco.

SERVES 4 | **TOTAL 25 MINUTES**

500g Brussels sprouts

50g Parmesan cheese, plus extra to serve

250g Greek yoghurt

½ a lemon

2 thick slices of sourdough bread

Trim and halve the Brussels, char in a large non-stick frying pan on a medium heat for 15 minutes, or until gnarly on the outside and steamy and tender on the inside, then tip on to a board. Meanwhile, finely grate most of the Parmesan and fold it through the yoghurt with the lemon juice. Season to taste with sea salt and black pepper, then spoon on to a serving platter.

Place the pan on a medium-high heat. Slice the bread into 1cm cubes and toast with a drizzle of olive oil for 4 minutes, or until golden, finely grating over the remaining Parmesan for the last few seconds, tossing occasionally. Arrange the croutons and Brussels on top of the yoghurt, and finish with extra shavings of Parmesan and a drizzle of extra virgin olive oil, tossing together just before serving.

ENERGY	FAT	SAT FAT	PROTEIN	CARBS	SUGARS	SALT	FIBRE
298kcal	9.4g	5.1g	19g	36.5g	6.4g	0.8g	4.7g

FANCY FIG SALAD
COTTAGE CHEESE, PATA NEGRA & HONEY DUKKAH PRALINE

The joy of my Mediterranean travels has inspired me to blend classic flavours like dukkah from Egypt with traditional Spanish ham, figs and honey, and bring them together in a surprising, delicious way.

SERVES 2 | **TOTAL 20 MINUTES**

4 tablespoons runny honey

2 tablespoons dukkah

1 x 250g tub of cottage cheese

4 perfectly ripe figs

50g Pata Negra or quality Spanish ham

Drizzle the honey into a pan over a medium heat and leave to bubble away for about 3 minutes, or until you've got a dark golden caramel – please don't be tempted to stir, taste or touch the mixture, just give the pan a gentle swirl occasionally. Meanwhile, lightly oil a piece of greaseproof paper, sprinkle the dukkah over a 15cm x 15cm area, then carefully pour the caramel over the top and it will naturally settle and cool. (To clean the pan effortlessly, pour in 2.5cm of water, pop the lid on and simmer for 5 minutes.) Once completely cool, snap up the praline and bash in a pestle and mortar until fine.

Divide the cottage cheese between two plates, quarter and scatter over the figs, and arrange the Pata Negra in and around the plate. Scatter over a few good pinches of the dukkah praline (save the rest in an airtight container for another day) and drizzle with extra virgin olive oil, to finish.

PS

If you don't fancy making the caramel, simply swap the honey for sesame snaps, and bash them to a powder with the dukkah.

ENERGY	FAT	SAT FAT	PROTEIN	CARBS	SUGARS	SALT	FIBRE
327kcal	10.9g	5.9g	25.8g	30.6g	26.3g	1.7g	6.2g

GRILLED FATTOUSH SALAD
SWEET ONION, PITTA BREAD & CUCUMBER, SUMAC DRESSING

Fattoush is a humble Lebanese salad, and here I've enjoyed twisting the flavours by quite brutally grilling the cucumber, onion and pitta, but then tossing them with a delicate sumac dressing.

SERVES 4 | **TOTAL 25 MINUTES**

1 heaped tablespoon sumac

3 red onions

2 cucumbers

320g mixed-colour cherry tomatoes

4 pittas

Place a griddle pan on a high heat. Drizzle 5 tablespoons of extra virgin olive oil and 2 tablespoons of red wine vinegar into a large shallow serving bowl, season with a pinch of sea salt and black pepper, mix in the sumac and put aside. Peel the onions and slice into 1cm rounds, then grill until softened and nicely charred on both sides, using tongs to transfer them straight to the dressing as you go.

Meanwhile, roughly peel the cucumbers, slice in half lengthways and use a teaspoon to scrape out and discard the seeds, then slice in half across the middle (to fit the pan). When there's space on the griddle, lay in the cucumber, turning until beautifully bar-marked. Remove to a board, crudely slice up, then add to the bowl. Quarter and add the tomatoes to the bowl. Slice the pittas into 1.5cm strips, then toast on the griddle. Toss everything together, season to perfection and serve straight away.

ENERGY	FAT	SAT FAT	PROTEIN	CARBS	SUGARS	SALT	FIBRE
383kcal	18.6g	2.6g	9.1g	43.5g	13.4g	1g	8.2g

SEARED SQUID SALAD
CRISPY BACON BITS, DRESSED CHICORY & GARLICKY TOASTS

There's no need for a boring salad, and for me this is super-fun, exciting and fast to make – think a bacon and squid-loaded surf and turf-style baguette, acting like a giant crouton on a sea of leaves.

SERVES 2 | **TOTAL 12 MINUTES**

2 rashers of smoked streaky bacon

2 cloves of garlic

300g whole squid, cleaned, gutted

½ a small rustic baguette (100g)

2 green chicory

Finely slice the bacon and peel and finely slice the garlic. Place the bacon in a large non-stick frying pan on a high heat with 1 tablespoon of olive oil and fry for 2 minutes, adding the garlic halfway and tossing regularly. Add the squid and a good pinch of black pepper and cook for a further 2 minutes, or until tender. Slice the squid into ½cm rings, roughly chopping the tentacles, then put back into the pan and toss together. Slice the baguette at a slight angle, then push the squid to one side of the pan and toast the bread until golden on both sides with all the lovely garlicky pan juices.

Meanwhile, trim and click off the chicory leaves, dress with 1 tablespoon each of extra virgin olive oil and red wine vinegar, and season to perfection. Divide the dressed chicory between plates, then pile the squid and crispy bacon on to the hot toasts and place on top.

ENERGY	FAT	SAT FAT	PROTEIN	CARBS	SUGARS	SALT	FIBRE
414kcal	18.8g	3.5g	30.6g	31.9g	2.3g	1.2g	1.4g

CHAR & CHOP SALAD
RIPE TOMATOES, FRESH DILL, GARLIC, CHILLI & FLATBREADS

Inspired by Palestinian Gazan dagga, I love that a few moments of charring and chopping tomatoes, plus a confident use of dill and seasoning, can transform the everyday into something extraordinary.

SERVES 4 | **TOTAL 30 MINUTES**

500g self-raising flour, plus extra for dusting

6 cloves of garlic

3 mixed-colour chillies

800g ripe mixed-colour tomatoes

1 bunch of dill (20g)

Put the flour in a bowl with a pinch of sea salt, then gradually add 300ml of water, mixing with a fork as you go. Tip on to a flour-dusted surface and knead for a few minutes until smooth, then cover and leave to rest. Place a large non-stick frying pan on a high heat. Peel and halve the garlic cloves and halve the chillies (deseed if you like), then place in the pan. Add the tomatoes, halving any larger ones, and remove everything to a large board once lightly charred – you may need to work in batches.

Cut the dough into quarters. One at a time, roll each piece out to a 30cm round, folding over the edges to create a crust, dusting with flour as you go. Cook in a large non-stick frying pan on a high heat until golden and puffed up on both sides. Repeat with the remaining dough, keeping the flatbreads warm under a clean tea towel until needed. Finely chop the charred garlic and chillies, then introduce most of the dill (stalks and all), followed by the tomatoes. Keep chopping and mixing to your desired consistency, then season to perfection with salt, black pepper, 2 teaspoons of red wine vinegar and 2 tablespoons of extra virgin olive oil. Serve on top of the flatbreads, and pick over the remaining dill.

ENERGY	FAT	SAT FAT	PROTEIN	CARBS	SUGARS	SALT	FIBRE
511kcal	8.3g	1.2g	13.1g	102.2g	8.2g	1.7g	6.3g

MOZZARELLA SALAD
RAW COURGETTES, CRISPY CAPERS, LEMON & CHILLI

This fast Italian-style salad is a perfect way to celebrate courgettes, teamed with flavour best friends lemon and chilli. Crispy capers add a warm pop of interest, and you can't go wrong with mozzarella.

SERVES 4 | **TOTAL 10 MINUTES**

2 tablespoons baby capers in brine

2 firm mixed-colour courgettes

2 lemons

2 mild red chillies

2 x 125g balls of buffalo mozzarella

Put a small non-stick frying pan on a medium heat. Once hot, go in with a little olive oil and the capers. Toss until crispy, while you coarsely grate the courgettes into the centre of a clean tea towel. Pull up the edges of the tea towel to make a bundle, wring out really well to remove the excess liquid, then transfer the courgettes to a serving bowl. Finely grate over the zest of 1 lemon, then squeeze over the juice from both lemons. Finely grate or slice the chillies and add to the mix. Drizzle with 2 tablespoons of extra virgin olive oil, toss together well, then season to perfection. Tear the mozzarella over the salad, spoon over the crispy capers, then sprinkle with an extra pinch of black pepper and serve – this salad is great in its own right, or with some hunks of crusty bread on the side.

ENERGY	FAT	SAT FAT	PROTEIN	CARBS	SUGARS	SALT	FIBRE
234kcal	19g	9.5g	13g	3.6g	2.9g	0.9g	1g

SOUPS & SARNIES

GREEN GAZPACHO
CUCUMBER, PEPPER, PARSLEY & PISTACHIOS

Vibrant, fresh and full of flavour, this take on the Spanish favourite gazpacho, a cold soup, is sure to hit the spot. Perfect for a light lunch, starter, supper, or just a moment of pure refreshment.

SERVES 4 | **TOTAL 15 MINUTES**

½ x 270g ciabatta loaf

1 bunch of flat-leaf parsley (30g)

100g shelled unsalted pistachios

1 cucumber

2 green peppers

Cut 8 thin slices of ciabatta, and toast until golden. Tear the remaining bread into a blender. Keep back a little of each of the remaining ingredients for garnish. Rip the parsley into the blender with the pistachios, chop and add the cucumber, and tear in the peppers, discarding the seeds and stalks.

Pour in 200ml of cold water along with 3 tablespoons each of extra virgin olive oil and red wine vinegar, then season well with sea salt and black pepper. Whiz together, then add 300g of ice and blitz again until silky smooth – you may need to work in batches. Taste and adjust the seasoning, if needed. Serve sprinkled with the reserved garnishes (leave whole or finely chop in a delicate fashion, whatever you prefer) and a drizzle of extra virgin olive oil, if you like. An extra ice cube or two is always a nice touch, too. Serve the crispy toasts alongside for dunking.

ENERGY	FAT	SAT FAT	PROTEIN	CARBS	SUGARS	SALT	FIBRE
244kcal	14.9g	2.1g	6.8g	21.6g	4.6g	0.8g	2.3g

BUTTER BEANS ON TOAST
CRISPY CHORIZO, FRESH PARSLEY & TANGY PEPPER SAUCE

Celebrating simple Spanish vibes, this vibrant dish really delivers on both speed and flavour. We're hero-ing big fat creamy butter beans, which teamed with chorizo and pepper sauce are a real joy.

SERVES 4 | **TOTAL 18 MINUTES**

1 x 460g jar of roasted red peppers

½ a bunch of flat-leaf parsley (15g)

1 small baguette (200g)

1 x 700g jar of giant butter beans or 2 x 400g tins of butter beans

170g chorizo

Place the peppers in a blender with 1 tablespoon of liquor from the jar. Tear off and reserve the top leafy half of the parsley, adding the stalks to the blender with 1 tablespoon of extra virgin olive oil. Blitz until smooth, then season to perfection with sea salt and black pepper. Cut the baguette into 8 slices and toast until golden. Put a non-stick frying pan on a high heat. Empty in the beans (juices and all), bring to the boil, then let the juices reduce until creamy, stirring occasionally.

Meanwhile, slice the chorizo ½cm thick, scatter into a non-stick frying pan and fry on a medium-high heat until golden and crisp, tossing regularly – it won't take long. Divide the pepper sauce between four plates or spread across a serving platter, sit the toasts on the sauce and spoon over the hot beans. Spoon the chorizo and its spicy juices over the beans, then dress the parsley leaves with a little extra virgin olive oil and red wine vinegar, and sprinkle over the top to finish.

ENERGY	FAT	SAT FAT	PROTEIN	CARBS	SUGARS	SALT	FIBRE
468kcal	17.5g	4.3g	23.2g	53.5g	9.1g	1.1g	9.5g

SIMPLE MARSEILLES FISH SOUP
BREAM, FENNEL & TOMATO BROTH, WARM CRUSTY BREAD & GARLIC MAYO

When you've got a beautiful whole fish, it doesn't need much to really shine. This method utilizes every part of the bream, with delicate flaky fish fillets as well as a flavoursome lip-smacking soup.

SERVES 2 | TOTAL 45 MINUTES

1 large bulb of fennel, ideally with leafy tops

600g ripe tomatoes

1 x 400g whole bream, scaled, gutted, gills removed

1 small baguette (200g)

2 tablespoons garlic mayo

Trim the fennel, reserving any leafy tops in a bowl of cold water. Remove and roughly chop the outer layers, and very finely slice the tender inner core as best you can. Add all the finely sliced fennel to the bowl of water, then place the rest in a large shallow casserole pan on a medium-high heat with 2 tablespoons of olive oil. Cook for 10 minutes, or until starting to caramelize, stirring regularly.

Roughly chop and add the tomatoes, then pour in 500ml of water. Bring to the boil, lay the fish on top, cover the pan and simmer gently for 10 minutes, turning the fish halfway. Remove the cooked fish to a plate, let it cool a little, then use two forks to lift the fillets away from the bones, discarding the skin and fins. Return all the bones and the head to the pan and boil on a high heat for 5 minutes. Carefully pour the entire contents of the pan into a blender and blitz until smooth, extracting maximum goodness and flavour, then season to perfection. Adjust the consistency to your liking with a splash of water, if needed, then push through a coarse sieve into warm soup bowls. Drain the fennel and dress with a little extra virgin olive oil and red wine vinegar. Serve with toasted bread, a blob of garlic mayo, the fish fillets and the dressed fennel. Finish with extra virgin olive oil, if you like.

ENERGY	FAT	SAT FAT	PROTEIN	CARBS	SUGARS	SALT	FIBRE
641kcal	22.3g	2.7g	35.3g	76.3g	12.4g	1.7g	11.2g

TOMATOES ON TOAST
HERBY GOAT'S CHEESE & CRUNCHY SMOKY ALMONDS

Stuffed with a creamy herby filling, then squashed into a rustic baguette, with a beautiful liquor for dunking, this humble dish is a celebration of beautiful bang-in-season tomatoes with a French twist.

SERVES 2 | **TOTAL 30 MINUTES**

4 really ripe round tomatoes (at room temperature)

20g smoked almonds

4 sprigs of curly parsley

70g soft goat's cheese

1 small rustic baguette (200g)

Use the tip of a knife to carefully cut the stalk away from the top of each tomato, then blanch in a pan of boiling water for 50 seconds. Drain and rinse under cold water, then carefully peel and discard the skin. Using your hand to hold each tomato in shape, carefully use a teaspoon to scoop the insides into a coarse sieve over a bowl. Push the juicy goodness through the sieve into the bowl, add a thimble of red wine vinegar, then season to perfection with sea salt and black pepper.

Bash most of the smoked almonds in a pestle and mortar until fine. Tear the top leafy half off the parsley and place in a bowl of ice-cold water. Finely chop the stalks and add to the bashed almonds with the goat's cheese, then mix together, loosening with a splash of water. Slice the baguette in half lengthways and toast until lightly golden. Meanwhile, spoon the cheese filling into a sandwich bag, cut off the corner and squeeze the filling into the tomatoes. Drizzle the inside of the toasted baguette with extra virgin olive oil, then place the tomatoes on the base. Drain the parsley well and toss with a little more oil, then scatter over the top. Finely chop and sprinkle over the remaining almonds, then pop the lid on and cut into slices. Serve with the tomato liquor, for dunking.

ENERGY	FAT	SAT FAT	PROTEIN	CARBS	SUGARS	SALT	FIBRE
469kcal	16.3g	5.9g	18g	60.6g	9.4g	1.3g	5.8g

MUSHROOM SOUP
SOUR CREAM RIPPLE, CRISPY MUSHROOMS

Inspired by the small but mighty Montenegro, where cooking is all about extracting maximum flavour from fresh local produce, this dark and delicious soup uses mushrooms in two exciting ways.

SERVES 4 | **TOTAL 30 MINUTES**

4 cloves of garlic

300g frozen chopped mixed onion, carrot and celery

750g chestnut mushrooms

1 litre chicken or vegetable stock

4 tablespoons sour cream

Preheat the oven to 180°C. Peel and finely slice the garlic, then place it in a large casserole pan on a medium-high heat with 2 tablespoons of olive oil and the frozen mixed veg. Fry for a few minutes while you slice 500g of the mushrooms, then add them to the pan with a good pinch of black pepper. Cook for 10 minutes, or until golden, then pour in the stock and cook for a further 10 minutes. Meanwhile, slice the remaining 250g of mushrooms (slice them so you have some beautiful cross-sections, throwing any trimmings into the soup as you go), place on a tray with a drizzle of olive oil and a pinch of sea salt and pepper, and roast for 15 minutes, or until beautifully golden and crisp.

When the time's up, blitz the soup to your desired consistency, then season to perfection. Divide between warm soup bowls, ripple 1 tablespoon of sour cream into each, and top with the crispy mushrooms and a little drizzle of extra virgin olive oil, if you like.

ENERGY	FAT	SAT FAT	PROTEIN	CARBS	SUGARS	SALT	FIBRE
189kcal	13.2g	3.5g	10.9g	5.8g	4.1g	0.8g	3.8g

EPIC TOMATO BREAD
CRISPY GARLIC & CHORIZO, MOLTEN MANCHEGO

Here, I'm celebrating a classic Spanish combo, but how I've put them together is definitely not typical. Super-fun and undeniably delicious, this is perfect served as part of a lunch or tapas spread.

SERVES 4 | **TOTAL 15 MINUTES**

100g chorizo

4 cloves of garlic

1 x 270g ciabatta loaf

400g ripe mixed-colour cherry tomatoes

100g Manchego cheese

Preheat the oven to 180°C. Slice the chorizo and peel and finely slice the garlic, place in a large non-stick ovenproof frying pan and toss with 1 tablespoon of olive oil, then place in the oven for 6 minutes, or until golden and caramelized. Carefully halve the ciabatta lengthways and warm alongside. Meanwhile, put half the tomatoes into a blender with 1 tablespoon of red wine vinegar and 2 tablespoons of extra virgin olive oil, season with sea salt and black pepper, then blitz. Push through a coarse sieve into a bowl. Quarter the remaining tomatoes and dress with just a little extra virgin olive oil, salt and red wine vinegar. Coarsely grate the Manchego.

Place the ciabatta spongy side up on a board, then spoon over and cover with the tomato sauce. Sprinkle over the dressed tomatoes, then divide over the chorizo and garlic, spooning most of the excess oil into a jam jar (for tasty cooking another day). Immediately sprinkle the cheese into the hot pan and allow the residual heat to gently melt it into a chorizo fondue. Pour directly over the bread as evenly as possible (your guests will go wild!), then slice up and serve.

ENERGY	FAT	SAT FAT	PROTEIN	CARBS	SUGARS	SALT	FIBRE
507kcal	31.8g	10.7g	19.5g	35.1g	7.3g	2.5g	3.4g

CRISPY SARDINE TOASTS
QUICK RED CABBAGE, FRESH CHILLI & FENNEL SEED PICKLE

I love the way these easy Istanbul-inspired sizzling sardine toasts get so crispy and the sardines cook right into the bread. Contrast with a cold, crunchy, quick pickle, and it's pure happiness on a plate.

SERVES 4 | **TOTAL 15 MINUTES**

1 heaped tablespoon fennel seeds

¼ of a red cabbage (320g)

1–2 mixed-colour chillies

1 x 270g ciabatta loaf

12 fresh sardines, scaled, gutted, butterflied

Toast the fennel seeds in a large non-stick frying pan on a medium heat for 1 minute, then pour in 2 tablespoons of olive oil, fry for 1 further minute and tip into a large bowl. Very finely slice or grate the red cabbage and chilli(es), and toss into the bowl with 4 tablespoons of red wine vinegar and a generous pinch of sea salt and black pepper. Leave aside to quickly pickle.

Carefully halve the ciabatta lengthways, drizzle with olive oil, then cut each half into 6 slices. Open out the sardines and firmly press on to the spongy side of each ciabatta slice, flesh side down. Preheat a griddle or non-stick frying pan to high, then place the toasts in the pan fish side down and cook for 2 minutes on each side, or until golden and crispy – you'll need to work in batches. Stack up 3 toasts per person and serve, with the fresh chilli and fennel seed pickle on top.

ENERGY	FAT	SAT FAT	PROTEIN	CARBS	SUGARS	SALT	FIBRE
462kcal	18.9g	4.1g	37.9g	38.2g	4.9g	1.6g	4.2g

BAKED TOMATO SOUP
SWEET PEPPERS, CIABATTA, RICOTTA, GARLIC

Thick bread soups are common all around Italy, but the baked versions really stand out for me — a real family favourite that everyone loves because it leaves you feeling warm, cosy and fulfilled.

SERVES 6 | TOTAL 1 HOUR

3 mixed-colour peppers

3 cloves of garlic

3 x 400g tins of plum tomatoes

1 x 270g ciabatta loaf (stale)

250g ricotta cheese

Preheat the oven to 180°C. Deseed the peppers and chop into 2cm chunks, then place in a large casserole pan on a medium heat with 2 tablespoons of olive oil and a pinch of sea salt and black pepper. Peel and finely slice the garlic, add to the pan, then reduce the heat to low and cook for 20 minutes, or until the peppers are soft and sweet, stirring regularly and adding splashes of water, if needed. Scrunch in the tomatoes through clean hands and pour in 2 tins' worth of water. Bring to the boil, while you slice the ciabatta 1cm thick. Stir the bread into the soup, then spoon over the ricotta and bake for 25 minutes, or until crisp on top and bubbling around the edges. Season to perfection, then divide between warm bowls and drizzle with a little extra virgin olive oil, if you like.

ENERGY	FAT	SAT FAT	PROTEIN	CARBS	SUGARS	SALT	FIBRE
288kcal	12.8g	5.1g	12g	31.6g	13.3g	0.8g	4.8g

SAUSAGE SANDWICH
MANCHEGO-STUFFED PEPPERS & OLIVE TAPENADE

It doesn't take a genius to work out that crispy golden sausage in a soft bun with sweet charred peppers stuffed with oozy Manchego cheese and fragrant tapenade is a great thing, any day. Enjoy!

SERVES 4 | TOTAL 18 MINUTES

4 brioche buns

6 sausages (400g total)

4 large jarred roasted red peppers (whole)

80g Manchego cheese

4 teaspoons black olive tapenade

Halve the brioche buns and quickly toast in a large dry non-stick frying pan on a medium-high heat, then put aside. Squeeze the sausages out of their skins into a bowl, then divide into 4 and with wet hands flatten out into 1cm-thick patties. Drizzle 1 tablespoon of olive oil into the pan, add the patties and cook for 2 minutes on each side, or until golden and cooked through, then remove to a plate. Meanwhile, drain the peppers and cut the Manchego into 4 slices (discarding any rind). Carefully stuff the peppers with the Manchego slices, then cook in the pan until starting to ooze, turning occasionally.

To serve, spread 1 teaspoon of olive tapenade over the base of each bun. Place a sausage patty on each one, then top with the Manchego-stuffed peppers and the bun lids, and get stuck in.

ENERGY	FAT	SAT FAT	PROTEIN	CARBS	SUGARS	SALT	FIBRE
577kcal	32.1g	11.6g	26.3g	44.1g	10.1g	2.6g	3.1g

TASTY CHICKPEA SOUP
MIXED SPICE, PLUM TOMATOES, BROKEN ODDS & ENDS PASTA

In Morocco they have a soup similar to this called harira, often eaten after a day of fasting. It's everything you want in a good soup — it's fulfilling and comforting, and made with humble ingredients.

SERVES 4 | **TOTAL 35 MINUTES**

300g frozen chopped mixed onion, carrot and celery

1 heaped teaspoon mixed spice, plus extra to serve

1 x 700g jar or 2 x 400g tins of chickpeas

2 x 400g tins of plum tomatoes

200g random leftover dried pasta

Tip the frozen mixed veg into a large, deep pan on a medium heat with 1 tablespoon of olive oil and the mixed spice. Cook for 10 minutes, or until golden, stirring regularly. Tip in the chickpeas (juices and all), then scrunch in the tomatoes through clean hands, followed by 2 tins' worth of water and the pasta, snapping any bigger bits as you go. Bring to the boil, then reduce to a simmer and leave to blip away for 20 minutes, or until thickened and reduced, stirring and mashing occasionally, and adding splashes of water, if needed. Season to perfection with sea salt and black pepper, and serve with a drizzle of extra virgin olive oil and an extra pinch of mixed spice, if you like.

ENERGY	FAT	SAT FAT	PROTEIN	CARBS	SUGARS	SALT	FIBRE
383kcal	7.3g	1g	16g	65.8g	10.4g	0.3g	8.8g

MY HOT MED SARNIE
JUICY CHICKEN, ROASTED RED PEPPERS, PESTO & BLACK OLIVES

When the bread is crisp, light and toasted in tasty pan juices, then covered in pesto and stuffed full of beautiful Mediterranean ingredients, you just know it's going to be off-the-chart on the flavour front.

SERVES 2 | **TOTAL 16 MINUTES**

4 skinless, boneless chicken thighs

1 small rustic baguette (200g)

1 large jarred roasted red pepper

8 black olives (stone in)

2 tablespoons pesto or pistou

Halve the chicken thighs, then season with sea salt and black pepper. Place in a large non-stick frying pan on a medium heat with ½ a tablespoon of olive oil and cook for 15 minutes, or until golden and cooked through, turning regularly. Slice the baguette in half lengthways and place in the pan to quickly toast and soak up all the tasty cooking juices. Drain the pepper and slice lengthways into slivers, destone and tear the olives, then add them both to the pan and cook for a couple of minutes, tossing occasionally. Spread the base of the baguette generously with the pesto. Pile the chicken and pepper filling on top, pop the lid on and squash and press down. Slice up, dig in and enjoy.

ENERGY	FAT	SAT FAT	PROTEIN	CARBS	SUGARS	SALT	FIBRE
610kcal	22.9g	4.9g	41.8g	57.5g	6g	1.8g	4.3g

PASTA

GREEK-CYPRIOT PASTA
ORZO, FRESH TOMATO, PARSLEY & HALLOUMI

My Greek-Cypriot sister, Georgie, got me on to this combo, and what a ray of sunshine it has brought to our kitchen table – the kids absolutely love it! Feel free to scatter in any delicate seasonal veg.

SERVES 2 | **TOTAL 26 MINUTES**

600g large ripe tomatoes

2 cloves of garlic

½ a bunch of flat-leaf parsley (15g)

200g dried orzo

40g halloumi cheese

Grate the tomatoes on to a plate using the fine side of a box grater, discarding any skin and seeds. Peel and slice the garlic, then place in a large non-stick frying pan on a medium heat with 2 tablespoons of olive oil and fry for 3 minutes, or until lightly golden. Meanwhile, pick a few pretty parsley leaves for garnish, then finely chop the rest (stalks and all) and add to the pan. Cook for 2 minutes, then tip in the tomatoes along with 500ml of water. Bring to the boil for a few minutes, then add the pasta and cook for a further 14 minutes, or until the pasta is just tender and the sauce has thickened, stirring regularly and adding splashes of water to loosen, if needed. Coarsely grate and stir through most of the halloumi, then taste and season to perfection with sea salt and black pepper. Grate over the remaining halloumi, scatter with the parsley leaves and drizzle with extra virgin olive oil, if you like.

ENERGY	FAT	SAT FAT	PROTEIN	CARBS	SUGARS	SALT	FIBRE
559kcal	19.7g	5.6g	18.9g	80.3g	10.1g	0.6g	5.7g

LEMONY ROCKET FARFALLE
SMASHED PISTACHIOS, PARMESAN & EXTRA VIRGIN OLIVE OIL

I've seen some incredible pasta sauces in the Sicilian islands made using pistachios, local cheeses and different herbs, such as rocket – finished with lemon, they're so vivid and packed full of flavour.

SERVES 6 | **TOTAL 15 MINUTES**

480g dried farfalle

120g rocket

2 lemons

100g Parmesan cheese, plus extra to serve

100g shelled unsalted pistachios

Cook the pasta in a pan of boiling salted water according to the packet instructions, then drain, reserving a mugful of starchy cooking water. Meanwhile, place most of the rocket in a blender, finely grate in the lemon zest and squeeze in all the juice. Drizzle in 6 tablespoons of extra virgin olive oil, then add the Parmesan, 2 tablespoons of starchy cooking water and most of the pistachios, and whiz until smooth. When the time's up, toss the pasta and sauce together, loosening with a splash of starchy cooking water, if needed. Finely chop the remaining pistachios and sprinkle the remaining rocket over the top. Finish with an extra grating of Parmesan and a drizzle of extra virgin olive oil.

ENERGY	FAT	SAT FAT	PROTEIN	CARBS	SUGARS	SALT	FIBRE
473kcal	21.2g	5.5g	16.3g	57.5g	2.2g	0.3g	0.7g

CHESTNUT CARBONARA
SMOKY PANCETTA, CREAMY PECORINO & BLACK PEPPER SAUCE

Oh my days, why has it taken me so long to infiltrate one of my favourite pasta dishes with beautiful chestnuts that can be nutty, crumbly and savoury, but sweet and smooth all at the same time.

SERVES 2 | **TOTAL 15 MINUTES**

150g random leftover dried pasta

3 rashers of smoked pancetta or streaky bacon

180g vac-packed chestnuts

4 large eggs

20g pecorino or Parmesan, plus extra to serve

Cook the pasta in a pan of boiling salted water according to the packet instructions, then drain, reserving a mugful of starchy cooking water. With 4 minutes to go, finely slice the pancetta and place in a large non-stick frying pan on a medium heat with 1 tablespoon of olive oil. Once sizzling, crumble in the chestnuts and add a generous pinch of black pepper, then stir regularly until golden and crisp.

Meanwhile, separate the eggs, putting the yolks into a bowl (save the whites for making meringues another day), then finely grate in the cheese and mix together. Tip the drained pasta into the chestnut pan, then remove from the heat and wait 2 minutes for the pan to cool slightly (if the pan's too hot, it'll scramble; get it right and it'll be smooth, silky and deliciously elegant). Loosen the egg mixture with a splash of the reserved cooking water, then pour over the pasta, tossing and stirring vigorously – the egg will gently cook in the residual heat. Season to perfection. Adjust the consistency with extra cooking water, if needed, and finish with a fine grating of cheese, if you like.

ENERGY	FAT	SAT FAT	PROTEIN	CARBS	SUGARS	SALT	FIBRE
726kcal	27.1g	7.6g	27.4g	97.7g	1.6g	1.2g	7.3g

TUNISIAN PRAWN SPAGHETTI
FRAGRANT ROSE HARISSA, ZINGY LEMON & FRESH PARSLEY

Tunisians are one of the biggest pasta eaters on the planet and they have a whole load of their own pasta shapes and techniques. Harissa really amplifies the sweetness of the prawns here – delicious!

SERVES 2 | **TOTAL 22 MINUTES**

150g dried spaghetti

8 large raw shell-on king prawns

2 teaspoons rose harissa

½ a bunch of flat-leaf parsley (15g)

1 lemon

Cook the pasta in a pan of boiling salted water according to the packet instructions. Meanwhile, peel the prawns, removing and reserving the heads and leaving the tails on. I like to run a small sharp knife down the back of each, discarding the vein, so they butterfly when they cook. Toss the prawns with the harissa and leave to briefly marinate. Place the prawn heads in a large frying pan on a medium heat with 1 tablespoon of olive oil and fry until golden all over, stirring regularly and gently squashing to extract amazing flavour. Roughly chop and reserve the top leafy half of the parsley, then finely slice the stalks and add them to the pan with a pinch of sea salt and black pepper. Fry for 1 minute, then add the marinated prawns and cook for 1 minute on each side. Using tongs, drag the pasta into the pan, squeeze in half the lemon juice, throw in the parsley leaves, then toss together, loosening with a splash of starchy cooking water, if needed. To serve, pick out and discard the crispy prawn heads and cut the remaining lemon half into wedges for squeezing over.

ENERGY	FAT	SAT FAT	PROTEIN	CARBS	SUGARS	SALT	FIBRE
373kcal	9.3g	1.2g	19.2g	56.3g	3.2g	0.9g	2.8g

ROASTED SQUASH LASAGNE
GOLDEN CHESTNUTS, OOZY TALEGGIO & FRAGRANT CRISPY SAGE

Stacking up the pasta sheets and turning them on their side gives this autumnal lasagne a truly wonderful texture. With crispy sage and toasted chestnuts in the mix too, it's a proper treat for the tastebuds.

SERVES 4 | **TOTAL 1 HOUR 45 MINUTES**

1 butternut or onion squash (1.2kg)

½ a bunch of sage (10g)

180g vac-packed chestnuts

10 fresh lasagne sheets (250g)

200g Taleggio cheese

Preheat the oven to 200°C. Carefully cut the squash in half lengthways, scoop out and discard the seeds, then rub all over with sea salt, black pepper and olive oil. Place flesh side up on a tray and roast for 1 hour, or until tender. Meanwhile, drizzle 2 tablespoons of olive oil into a non-stick frying pan on a medium heat, pick in the sage leaves and cook until crispy, then remove to kitchen paper. Add the chestnuts to the pan, tossing regularly and removing when lightly golden and crisp.

When the squash is done, lay the 10 pasta sheets out on a flat surface, then break up, scoop and divide the squash flesh on to the pasta. Crumble over most of the chestnuts and tear over most of the cheese, then stack up and lightly press together 5 sheets, and repeat. Slice each stack lengthways into 3 strips and arrange sideways in an oiled 20cm x 20cm baking dish. Pour over 150ml of boiling kettle water. Crumble over the remaining chestnuts and tear over the remaining cheese. Cover with tin foil and bake for 30 minutes, or until golden and cooked through, removing the foil halfway and topping with the crispy sage leaves for the final 5 minutes. Finish with a drizzle of extra virgin olive oil, if you like.

ENERGY	FAT	SAT FAT	PROTEIN	CARBS	SUGARS	SALT	FIBRE
604kcal	23.3g	10.2g	18.8g	81g	14.2g	2.3g	11.5g

GREEK CHICKEN PASTA
SWEET TOMATO SAUCE, MACARONI & GRATED HALLOUMI

On the Greek island of Andros they serve variations of this undeniably delicious pasta — it's the easiest thing to put together and the Oliver squad loves it (the teenagers thought the halloumi was peng!).

SERVES 8 | **TOTAL 1 HOUR 30 MINUTES**

1kg chicken thighs, skin on, bone in

500g frozen chopped mixed onion, carrot and celery

2 x 400g tins of plum tomatoes

600g dried macaroni

100g halloumi cheese

Brown the chicken thighs all over in a large non-stick casserole pan on a high heat with 2 tablespoons of olive oil, then remove to a plate. Tip in the frozen mixed veg and soften for 5 minutes, then put the chicken back into the pan with 2 tablespoons of red wine vinegar and allow it to cook away. Scrunch in the tomatoes through clean hands, then pour in 1 tin's worth of water. Bring to the boil, then leave to blip away on a low heat for 1 hour, or until the chicken is falling off the bone, stirring occasionally.

When the time's up, cook the pasta in a pan of boiling salted water according to the packet instructions, then drain. Meanwhile, strip all the chicken meat from the bones and shread apart with forks, returning it to the sauce as you go and discarding any skin and bones. Taste the sauce and season to perfection. To serve, stir the pasta into the sauce and grate in most of the halloumi. Finish drizzled with 1 tablespoon of extra virgin olive oil and with the remaining halloumi grated over the top.

ENERGY	FAT	SAT FAT	PROTEIN	CARBS	SUGARS	SALT	FIBRE
566kcal	19.5g	5.7g	40.5g	60g	4.4g	0.8g	1.4g

SWEET PEA ORECCHIETTE
BROKEN POTATOES, SPRING ONIONS & GRATED PECORINO

My family love the southern Italian orecchiette pasta shape – perfect for catching the gorgeous sweet peas – and the double carb hit of diced potato with tangy pecorino and olive oil is blissful.

SERVES 4 | **TOTAL 30 MINUTES**

600g potatoes

1 bunch of spring onions

320g frozen peas

300g dried orecchiette

80g pecorino cheese, plus extra to serve

Peel the potatoes and chop into 1cm cubes, trim and slice the spring onions, then place in a large non-stick frying pan on a high heat with 2 tablespoons of olive oil and 250ml of boiling kettle water. Reduce to a simmer, then cover and cook for 15 minutes, or until the potatoes are just tender, adding the peas for the last 5 minutes, stirring occasionally. Meanwhile, cook the pasta in a pan of boiling salted water according to the packet instructions, then drain, reserving a mugful of starchy cooking water. Tip the drained pasta into the pea and potato pan, finely grate in the pecorino, then toss together, adding splashes of cooking water to loosen, if needed. Season to perfection, and finish with an extra grating of pecorino and a drizzle of extra virgin olive oil, if you like.

ENERGY	FAT	SAT FAT	PROTEIN	CARBS	SUGARS	SALT	FIBRE
577kcal	15.9g	5.7g	21.9g	92.4g	5g	0.9g	6.6g

CRAB MEATBALLS
LINGUINE & ARRABBIATA SAUCE

The Mediterraneans love to make meatballs using all kinds of fish and seafood. I've used delicate picked crab in this tasty pasta – it's super-easy to make and feels really special and impressive. Yum!

SERVES 2 | **TOTAL 20 MINUTES**

1 large egg

1 picked dressed crab or 2 x 100g tubs of 50/50 crabmeat

100g fresh breadcrumbs

150g dried linguine

½ x 400g jar of arrabbiata sauce

Crack the egg into a bowl, add the crabmeat and breadcrumbs, then scrunch and mix together and roll into 16 balls. Cook the pasta in a pan of boiling salted water according to the packet instructions. Meanwhile, drizzle 1 tablespoon of olive oil into a large non-stick frying pan on a medium-high heat, then add the balls and cook for 6 minutes, or until golden all over, jiggling the pan occasionally for even cooking. Push the balls to one side of the pan, tip in the arrabbiata sauce, then bring to the boil for 2 minutes, keeping the pan moving. Use tongs to drag the pasta straight into the pan, letting a little starchy cooking water go with it, then toss everything together, loosening with extra splashes of water, if needed. Season to perfection, and finish with a drizzle of extra virgin olive oil, if you like.

ENERGY	FAT	SAT FAT	PROTEIN	CARBS	SUGARS	SALT	FIBRE
638kcal	17.9g	3g	37g	85.1g	8.3g	1.6g	3.3g

TURKISH-INSPIRED PASTA
GOLDEN GARLICKY LAMB, CREAMY YOGHURT & FRAGRANT MINT

Utterly delicious, these ingredients are not things I ever thought would work in combination with pasta, but this dish is pungent yet fragrant, and the comforting flavours are both familiar and surprising.

SERVES 4 | **TOTAL 25 MINUTES**

400g minced lamb

4 cloves of garlic

1 bunch of mint (30g)

300g dried tubular pasta, such as gomiti or macaroni

250g natural yoghurt

Place the minced lamb in a large non-stick frying pan on a medium-low heat with 1 tablespoon of olive oil and fry for 3 minutes, or until browned all over. Peel and finely chop 3 cloves of garlic and add to the pan, followed by 1 tablespoon of red wine vinegar, a splash of water, a pinch of sea salt and lots of black pepper. Cook for a further 5 minutes, stirring regularly, then mash with a potato masher to soften. Pick the baby mint leaves and reserve for garnish, then pick and finely chop the rest and add to the pan. Reduce the heat to low and leave to tick away while you cook the pasta in a pan of boiling salted water according to the packet instructions.

Peel and finely grate the remaining garlic clove, mix with the yoghurt and season with a pinch of salt and pepper. Drain the pasta, reserving a mugful of starchy cooking water, then tip the pasta straight into the lamb pan. Cook for 1 minute, then add the garlicky yoghurt and toss together, loosening with a splash of cooking water, if needed. Sprinkle over the reserved mint leaves, to serve.

ENERGY	FAT	SAT FAT	PROTEIN	CARBS	SUGARS	SALT	FIBRE
542kcal	20.5g	8.5g	31.3g	62g	5.7g	0.9g	0.3g

MUSSEL TAGLIATELLE
GARLIC, MUSHROOMS, MANCHEGO & FRESH-CUT PASTA

Across the Mediterranean I've witnessed a number of dishes featuring the beautiful marriage of mushrooms and seafood – there's just something so delicious and delicate about it, you have to try it.

SERVES 2 | TOTAL 15 MINUTES

4 portobello mushrooms (250g)

2 cloves of garlic

600g mussels, scrubbed, debearded

250g fresh lasagne sheets

40g Manchego cheese, plus extra to serve

Peel the mushrooms and slice ½cm thick, then place in a dry non-stick casserole pan on a high heat with the lid on and cook for 3 minutes, shaking regularly, while you peel and finely slice the garlic. Remove the lid, add 2 tablespoons of olive oil and the garlic, then season with sea salt and black pepper. Cook for 3 minutes, while you check the mussels – if any are open, give them a tap and they should close; if they don't, discard them. Slice the lasagne sheets lengthways into 1cm strips and boil the kettle.

Stir the mussels and pasta into the pan with just enough boiling kettle water to cover the pasta (about 350ml), then pop the lid on and let it bubble away for around 4 minutes, or until the mussels have opened and are soft and juicy, shaking the pan occasionally. If any remain closed, discard them. Coarsely grate the cheese into the pan, toss together, and season to perfection. Divide between bowls, and serve with an extra grating of Manchego and a drizzle of extra virgin olive oil, if you like.

ENERGY	FAT	SAT FAT	PROTEIN	CARBS	SUGARS	SALT	FIBRE
530kcal	25.9g	7.3g	29.2g	43.9g	1.5g	1.2g	4.6g

SPEEDY TUNA PASTA
SWEET CHERRY TOMATOES, FRAGRANT BASIL & CHILLI

Tomato and basil is a flavour combo that transports me straight to the islands of Italy. Teamed with super-fresh tuna and a chilli heat, this simple pasta will have you dreaming of balmy summer nights.

SERVES 2 | TOTAL 14 MINUTES

150g dried spaghetti

1 fresh red chilli

160g ripe mixed-colour cherry tomatoes

1 x 150g tuna steak

½ a bunch of basil (15g)

Cook the pasta in a pan of boiling salted water according to the packet instructions. Meanwhile, finely slice the chilli, tomatoes, tuna steak and basil leaves (reserving a few baby leaves for garnish), and scrape into a large serving bowl. Add 2 tablespoons of extra virgin olive oil and 1 tablespoon of red wine vinegar, mix well, then season to perfection with sea salt and black pepper. Once the pasta is cooked, use tongs to drag it straight into the bowl, letting a splash of starchy cooking water go with it. Toss until well mixed, loosening with an extra splash of cooking water, if needed – the residual heat of the steamy pasta will start to delicately cook the tuna, just enough to give you a truly elegant dish. Scatter over the reserved basil leaves and serve with a drizzle of extra virgin olive oil, if you like.

ENERGY	FAT	SAT FAT	PROTEIN	CARBS	SUGARS	SALT	FIBRE
496kcal	18.2g	3g	27.8g	58.7g	5.2g	0.4g	3g

MOROCCAN PASTA
ARTICHOKES, MARINATED OLIVES, GARLIC & TOMATOES

On my travels in Morocco I was happily surprised to see angel hair pasta used in many different ways – not just in stews and simple pasta dishes like this, but also as stuffings and side dishes.

SERVES 2 | **TOTAL 15 MINUTES**

150g vermicelli or angel hair pasta

75g mixed marinated olives

2 cloves of garlic

½ x 280g jar of artichoke hearts in oil

1 x 400g tin of plum tomatoes

Cook the vermicelli or angel hair pasta in a pan of boiling salted water according to the packet instructions, then drain, reserving a mugful of starchy cooking water. Meanwhile, destone the olives (if needed), peel and finely chop the garlic, place them in a large non-stick frying pan (including the olive marinade ingredients) on a medium heat with the artichokes and 2 tablespoons of the oil from the artichoke jar, and fry until lightly golden. Crush and push the tomatoes through a coarse sieve into the pan, and season to perfection with sea salt and black pepper. Simmer for a few minutes, then toss the vermicelli or pasta and sauce together, loosening with a splash of cooking water, if needed.

ENERGY	FAT	SAT FAT	PROTEIN	CARBS	SUGARS	SALT	FIBRE
548kcal	24.3g	3.4g	9.4g	72.6g	7.9g	1.8g	5.3g

ASPARAGUS CARBONARA
SMOKED PANCETTA, EGG YOLKS, BLACK PEPPER & PECORINO

I never get bored cooking this dish – it comes together so effortlessly. I just love the contrast between the dark peppery pancetta and delicate asparagus, all coated in the silky egg and cheese sauce.

SERVES 4 | **TOTAL 15 MINUTES**

300g dried penne

350g asparagus

4 large eggs

50g pecorino or Parmesan, plus extra to serve

4 rashers of smoked pancetta or streaky bacon

Cook the pasta in a large pan of boiling salted water according to the packet instructions. Meanwhile, snap the woody ends off the asparagus, then slice the stalks roughly the same length as the pasta, halving any thick stalks lengthways. Separate the eggs, putting the yolks into a bowl (save the whites for making meringues another day), then finely grate in the cheese and mix together.

Finely slice the pancetta, then place in a large non-stick frying pan on a medium-high heat with 1 tablespoon of olive oil and a generous pinch of black pepper and cook for 4 minutes, or until golden and crisp. Add the asparagus to the pancetta for 3 minutes, then drain the pasta, reserving a mugful of starchy cooking water. Tip the pasta into the pancetta pan, toss and stir everything together, then remove from the heat and wait 2 minutes for the pan to cool slightly (if the pan's too hot, it'll scramble; get it right and it'll be smooth, silky and deliciously elegant). Loosen the egg mixture with a splash of cooking water, then pour over the pasta, tossing and stirring vigorously – the egg will gently cook in the residual heat. Season to perfection. Adjust the consistency with extra cooking water, if needed, and finish with a pinch of pepper and an extra grating of cheese, if you like.

ENERGY	FAT	SAT FAT	PROTEIN	CARBS	SUGARS	SALT	FIBRE
463kcal	17.5g	5.7g	22.2g	58.4g	3.3g	1.1g	1.5g

VEG

SMOKY TENDER AUBERGINE
SILKEN HOUMOUS, CRISPY CHICKPEAS, RADISHES & LEMON

Vibing off flavours from the Levantine coast, I'm using chickpeas in two different ways to max out on both flavour and texture. Peeled blackened aubergine adds a smoky depth that's hard to beat.

SERVES 2 | **TOTAL 22 MINUTES**

2 aubergines (250g each)

50g sesame seeds

½ x 700g jar or 1 x 400g tin of chickpeas

2 lemons

200g radishes, ideally with leaves

Prick the aubergines, then carefully blacken them over a direct flame on the hob (or under the grill), turning with tongs until soft inside. Meanwhile, toast the sesame seeds in a large non-stick frying pan on a high heat until golden, tossing regularly. Put two-thirds of the toasted seeds into a blender, saving the rest for later. Drain the chickpeas (reserving the juice) and add two-thirds to the blender with the juice of 1 lemon and 2 tablespoons of extra virgin olive oil. Blitz until super-smooth, loosening with splashes of chickpea juice, if needed, then season to perfection and divide between plates.

Halve the radishes, toss with the remaining lemon juice and season with sea salt to quickly pickle. Once cool enough to handle, carefully remove the aubergine skin, then halve lengthways leaving them intact at the stalk, and season with salt and black pepper. Return the frying pan to a medium heat with a drizzle of olive oil, and scatter in the remaining chickpeas. Push the chickpeas to one side, then add the aubergines and cook for 5 minutes, or until the chickpeas are golden and crispy and the aubergine is starting to caramelize, turning as needed. Divide between plates, scatter over the reserved toasted sesame seeds and radishes, and finish with a drizzle of extra virgin olive oil, if you like.

ENERGY	FAT	SAT FAT	PROTEIN	CARBS	SUGARS	SALT	FIBRE
446kcal	31.4g	5.3g	15.3g	26.3g	8.1g	0.5g	5.6g

ROGUE RATATOUILLE RISOTTO
GRILLED MEDITERRANEAN VEG, FRAGRANT BASIL & TANGY GOAT'S CHEESE

I love this quick and simple one-pan dish with a passion — it's a crowd-pleaser, bringing Italy and Provence together. Purists would judge the frozen veg base hack, but I guarantee they're missing out.

SERVES 4 | **TOTAL 35 MINUTES**

700g frozen chargrilled Mediterranean veg

300g risotto rice

1.2 litres chicken or vegetable stock

1 bunch of basil (30g)

100g goat's cheese

Tip the frozen veg into a large, deep pan on a medium-high heat with 2 tablespoons of olive oil. Cook for 10 minutes, or until soft, stirring regularly, then remove half to a bowl. Add the rice to the pan and stir for 2 minutes. Add ladlefuls of hot stock and wait until each has been fully absorbed before adding another, stirring constantly for 16 to 18 minutes, or until the rice is perfectly cooked, adding extra splashes of water, if needed. Pick and finely slice most of the basil leaves and stir into the pan with the reserved veg, most of the goat's cheese and 1 tablespoon of extra virgin olive oil, and season to perfection. Adjust the consistency so it's nice and oozy with a splash of boiling kettle water, if needed. Divide between plates, then scatter over the remaining basil leaves and goat's cheese, to finish.

ENERGY	FAT	SAT FAT	PROTEIN	CARBS	SUGARS	SALT	FIBRE
610kcal	17.3g	5.4g	21g	92.5g	17.6g	0.6g	8.6g

GLORIOUS STUFFED SQUASH
MIXED HERBY GRAINS, OOZY CODDLED EGG & HARISSA DRESSING

Inspired by my travels to North Africa and their love for stuffed veg, this dish brings drama to the table, where you break and mix the oozy egg through the herby grain filling just before devouring.

SERVES 2 | **TOTAL 1 HOUR 15 MINUTES**

1 squash, such as kabocha, Crown Prince, onion, butternut (1.2kg)

1 bunch of flat-leaf parsley (30g)

1 x 250g packet of cooked mixed grains

2 large eggs

2 heaped teaspoons harissa

Preheat the oven to 180°C. Carefully cut the squash in half, scoop out and discard the seeds, then trim the ends and rub all over with sea salt, black pepper and olive oil. Place in a roasting tray, flesh side up, and roast for 50 minutes, or until tender (if you're using a butternut squash, scoop some soft flesh out to make a gully for the grains all along the length of the squash). Pick and finely chop the parsley, then toss most of it with the grains, along with 1 heaped teaspoon of harissa (and any extra butternut squash flesh, if using). Season with a pinch of salt and pepper, then divide between the squash halves. Make a well in the middle and crack an egg into each, then bake for 15 minutes for an oozy egg, or a little longer, if you prefer. Mix the remaining harissa with enough boiling kettle water to loosen, then drizzle over the squash and scatter over the remaining chopped parsley, to serve. At the table, break and mix the oozy egg through the grains, and tuck in.

ENERGY	FAT	SAT FAT	PROTEIN	CARBS	SUGARS	SALT	FIBRE
547kcal	13.9g	2.6g	20.6g	86.8g	29g	1.7g	14.6g

POTATO BOMBAS
CRISPY CRUMB, OOZY MANCHEGO & SPICY TOMATO SAUCE

I tried a secret recipe for potato bombas at a famous breakfast restaurant called La Cova Fumada in Barcelona, and wanted to create my own version, turning the humble potato into a thing of wonder.

SERVES 6 | **TOTAL 45 MINUTES**

4 large potatoes (1kg)

2 large eggs

150g Manchego cheese

100g fresh breadcrumbs

1 x 400g jar of arrabbiata sauce

Prick the potatoes all over with a fork and microwave on high for 30 minutes, or until tender, turning halfway. Once cool enough to handle, halve and scrape the insides into a bowl. Mash until smooth and season to perfection. Separate the eggs, putting the whites into a shallow bowl. Add the yolks to the potatoes and mash to combine. Chop most of the Manchego into 1cm cubes, then work into the mash mixture. Beat the egg whites. Divide the mash mixture into 6 and roll into balls, flattening slightly. Dip in the beaten egg whites, allowing any excess to drip off, then roll in breadcrumbs to coat.

Pour 1cm of olive oil into a non-stick frying pan over a medium-high heat. Once hot, carefully add the potato bombas and cook for 6 minutes, or until beautifully golden, turning halfway – you may need to work in batches. Meanwhile, heat the spicy arrabbiata sauce in a pan. Divide between plates and place the bombas on top, finely grate over the remaining Manchego, season to taste with sea salt and black pepper, and drizzle over a little extra virgin olive oil, if you like.

ENERGY	FAT	SAT FAT	PROTEIN	CARBS	SUGARS	SALT	FIBRE
336kcal	13.6g	6g	13.7g	41.1g	4.6g	1g	2.5g

MY MUJADARA
SPICED LENTILS & BULGUR, CRISPY ONIONS & YOGHURT

A much-loved and relied-on frugal Levantine dish, mujadara is outrageously tasty for the simplicity of its preparation and can be embellished with seasonal veg and leftover cooked meat, if you have it.

SERVES 4 | **TOTAL 45 MINUTES**

2 large onions

2 heaped tablespoons cumin seeds

150g dried brown lentils

150g bulgur wheat

4 tablespoons natural yoghurt

Put a small sturdy saucepan on a medium-high heat and pour in 2cm of olive oil. Peel and very finely slice 1 onion, then deep-fry until nicely golden and crisp, and drain on kitchen paper – you'll need to work in batches. To check the oil is up to temperature, add a piece of onion – it's ready once the onion turns golden and floats (or when the oil reaches 180°C on a thermometer).

Meanwhile, peel and chop the remaining onion, place in a large non-stick frying pan on a medium heat, along with the cumin seeds and 1 tablespoon of olive oil, and fry for 10 minutes, or until sweet and soft. Add the lentils, bulgur and 1.2 litres of water, bring to the boil, then simmer for 25 minutes, or until the lentils and bulgur are cooked and almost all the water has been absorbed. Taste and season to perfection with sea salt and black pepper, then fold through half the crispy onions. Divide between plates, and top with dollops of yoghurt and the remaining crispy onions.

PS
If you don't fancy deep-frying, you can buy crispy onions ready-done from most supermarkets.

ENERGY	FAT	SAT FAT	PROTEIN	CARBS	SUGARS	SALT	FIBRE
408kcal	16g	2.7g	15.5g	56g	7.9g	0.1g	8.1g

RUNNER BEAN STEW
SWEET TOMATO, GARLIC & OREGANO SAUCE, TANGY CHEESE

I think a lot of people get stuck in a rut with how they cook their beans, but stewing them with simple flavours can give you something exciting to beautifully complement meat, fish or other veg dishes.

SERVES 4 | **TOTAL 45 MINUTES**

400g runner beans

2 cloves of garlic

½ a bunch of oregano (10g)

2 x 400g tins of plum tomatoes

100g feta cheese

Preheat the oven to 180°C. Trim the beans and speed-peel the sides to remove any tough stringy bits. Peel and finely slice the garlic, then place in a large casserole or ovenproof frying pan on a medium heat with 2 tablespoons of olive oil. Pick in the oregano, and cook until the garlic is very lightly golden, stirring regularly. Add the tomatoes, breaking them up with a potato masher, and season with a pinch of sea salt and black pepper. Bring to a simmer, then lay in the beans, pushing them down into the sauce. Cover with a scrunched-up piece of wet greaseproof, place in the oven for 30 minutes, or until the beans are tender and the sauce has thickened, then remove the paper. Crumble over the feta and either serve straight away or place in the oven for a final 10 minutes – the choice is yours.

ENERGY	FAT	SAT FAT	PROTEIN	CARBS	SUGARS	SALT	FIBRE
183kcal	12.2g	4.5g	7.9g	11.6g	10.8g	1.1g	1.8g

MINTY COURGETTE TART
GOLDEN FLAKY PASTRY, BLACK OLIVE TAPENADE & GOAT'S CHEESE

Inspired by cooking amazing courgettes with a wonderful Syrian lady called Majda, who had fled to Marseille and started up an incredible restaurant, this is my unconventional take on a pissaladière.

SERVES 4 TO 6 | **TOTAL 1 HOUR 35 MINUTES**

1.5kg courgettes

1 heaped teaspoon dried mint

320g sheet of ready-rolled puff pastry (cold)

6 teaspoons black olive tapenade

80g goat's cheese

Trim and peel the courgettes, quarter lengthways, cut away and discard the seedy core, then roughly chop and place in a large shallow casserole pan on a medium heat with 2 tablespoons of olive oil and the dried mint. Cook gently for 30 minutes, stirring regularly, then mash half the courgettes with a potato masher and fold back through the rest. Season to perfection and leave to cool for 5 minutes.

Preheat the oven to 200°C. Unroll the pastry sheet on its paper and place on a baking tray. Spoon over the cooled courgettes, leaving a 1cm border around the edge, then fold up the sides, pressing at the corners to secure. Brush the exposed pastry with a little oil, and cook at the bottom of the oven for 30 minutes, or until the pastry is beautifully golden and puffed up. Randomly dot over the olive tapenade, break over the fresh goat's cheese, then take to the table and serve up.

PS

If you want to use courgette flowers, like I have in the picture, have a go at growing them yourself (it's really easy!), or buy them from farmers' markets, as you'll rarely find them in supermarkets. Simply open them out, arrange on top of the tart and drizzle with a little oil before baking.

ENERGY	FAT	SAT FAT	PROTEIN	CARBS	SUGARS	SALT	FIBRE
584kcal	41.8g	15.8g	15.9g	50.9g	7.5g	1.3g	5.4g

SQUASH TAGINE
CREAMY CHICKPEAS, RAS EL HANOUT, OLIVES & DATES

Hero-ing the humble squash, I've cooked this Moroccan-inspired tagine in a casserole pan to make it more accessible, but please use a tagine if you have one. The dates melt to create an incredible sauce.

SERVES 4 | **TOTAL 1 HOUR**

1 butternut squash (1.2kg)

100g Medjool dates

1 tablespoon ras el hanout, plus extra for dusting

1 x 700g jar or 2 x 400g tins of chickpeas

100g marinated green olives

Scrub the squash, then carefully halve lengthways and chop into 4cm chunks, roughly chopping the seeds (I like to leave the skin on because it's nutty and delicious). Place the seeds in a large shallow casserole pan on a medium-high heat with a little drizzle of olive oil, tossing regularly – as soon as they start to pop, scoop them into a small bowl. Put the squash in the pan with 1 tablespoon of olive oil, and spend 10 minutes letting it get beautifully brown on each side, turning with tongs. Meanwhile, destone the dates and place in a bowl with 500ml of boiling kettle water.

Stir the ras el hanout into the pan, then pour in the chickpeas (juice and all) and add the dates and their soaking water. Tear in the olives (destone, if needed), then cover and cook for 20 minutes. Remove the lid, and let it simmer and reduce to a thick consistency – about 5 minutes (give it an extra 5 minutes if using tinned chickpeas). Season to perfection, then sprinkle over the crispy seeds and an extra pinch of ras el hanout. Serve as is, or with steamed couscous or bread on the side.

ENERGY	FAT	SAT FAT	PROTEIN	CARBS	SUGARS	SALT	FIBRE
347kcal	11g	1.7g	12g	51.9g	22.3g	1.1g	11.3g

CUCUMBER FRITTERS
SUPER-CRISP BATTER, CHEAT'S TZATZIKI & LEMON

These little morsels are wonderful, and make a fantastic starter or meze. What's brilliant here is that you can elevate cucumber to a whole other level, but you can also swap in other seasonal veg.

SERVES 4 (2 FRITTERS EACH) | **TOTAL 25 MINUTES**

2 cucumbers

75g gluten-free self-raising flour

300g Greek yoghurt

1 lemon

½ x 460g jar of roasted red peppers

Coarsely grate the cucumbers into a bowl, then add ½ a teaspoon of sea salt and toss together. Leave aside for 15 minutes, then squeeze out and discard as much liquid as you can. Tip the flour (I like to use gluten-free here for a lighter batter) into a separate bowl, and add 100g of yoghurt, a pinch of black pepper and 2 tablespoons of water. Finely grate in half the lemon zest and whisk together until smooth, then fold through half the cucumber.

Place a non-stick frying pan on a medium-high heat, pour in ½cm of olive oil and leave for a few minutes. Once hot, carefully add 8 heaped tablespoons of the batter and cook for 4 minutes, or until golden and cooked through, carefully flipping halfway – you may need to work in batches. Remove to kitchen paper to drain. Meanwhile, mix the rest of the cucumber with the rest of the yoghurt, finely grate in the remaining lemon zest, squeeze in half the juice and season with a pinch of salt and pepper, then divide between four plates. Drain the roasted peppers, then finely slice and dress with a little red wine vinegar and extra virgin olive oil. Scatter a pinch of dressed pepper over each plate and top with a couple of fritters. Slice the zested lemon into wedges for squeezing over, and get stuck in.

ENERGY	FAT	SAT FAT	PROTEIN	CARBS	SUGARS	SALT	FIBRE
260kcal	14.8g	4.2g	9.8g	21.7g	6.6g	1.1g	2g

HOME-STYLE KAFTEJI
HARISSA ROAST VEG, GOLDEN POTATOES & FRIED EGGS

The sound of Tunisian kafteji being chopped in the streets is epic. Typically the vegetables are deep-fried, which not everyone has access to, so this is my healthier, oven-version of this great dish.

SERVES 2 | **TOTAL 50 MINUTES**

2 green peppers

2 large ripe tomatoes

500g Maris Piper potatoes

1 tablespoon harissa or rose harissa, plus extra to serve

2 large eggs

Preheat the oven to 200°C. Trim, halve and deseed the peppers and halve the tomatoes, then place them in a large roasting tray, cut side up. Season with sea salt and black pepper, then roast for 35 minutes, or until tender. Meanwhile, scrub the potatoes and slice in half lengthways, then again into ½cm moons. Dress with 1 tablespoon of olive oil, season to taste, then spread out in a single layer on a large baking tray and roast for 25 minutes, or until golden and crisp. When the time's up on the peppers and tomatoes, chop them until fine, discarding any tough skin. Scrape into a bowl, dress with the harissa and season to taste with salt, pepper and red wine vinegar. Fry the eggs to your liking and serve on the side, along with the crispy potatoes. Drizzle with a little harissa, to taste, and tuck in.

ENERGY	FAT	SAT FAT	PROTEIN	CARBS	SUGARS	SALT	FIBRE
380kcal	15.3g	2.8g	13.9g	50.4g	8.3g	0.9g	4.5g

AUBERGINE FLATBREADS
HOT MARINATED OLIVES, TANGY FETA & DRIED OREGANO

Inspired by the flatbread work I've seen in Greek and Turkish street food, this makes a delicious lunch. It's a super-quick dough, plus blackening aubergines gives them the most extraordinary flavour.

SERVES 2 | **TOTAL 25 MINUTES**

1 large aubergine (400g)

200g self-raising flour, plus extra for dusting

10 mixed marinated olives

2 sprigs or 1 heaped teaspoon dried flowering oregano

50g feta cheese

Prick the aubergine, carefully blacken over a direct flame on the hob (or under the grill), turning with tongs until soft inside, then place in a bowl to cool. Meanwhile, put the flour in a bowl with a pinch of sea salt, then gradually add 100ml of water, mixing with a fork as you go. Tip on to a flour-dusted surface and knead for a few minutes until smooth, then cover and leave to briefly rest. Dust the surface with more flour, then split the dough in half and roll each piece out into an oval shape, roughly 20cm long. Place a large non-stick pan on a high heat, then lay in the dough and cook for 2½ minutes on each side, or until golden and cooked through – you'll need to work in batches. Meanwhile, chop the olives (destone, if needed), plus any of the marinating ingredients.

Once you've cooked the flatbreads, put the pan back on a very low heat. Leaving the juices in the bowl, slice the aubergine in half lengthways, then use a teaspoon to scrape out the flesh into the bowl, discarding any skin. Add 1 tablespoon each of extra virgin olive oil and red wine vinegar and half the oregano. Stir and break up with a spoon, then season to perfection with salt and black pepper. Spoon the dressed aubergine on to the flatbreads. Scatter the chopped olives into the pan with 1 tablespoon of olive oil, allow to sizzle for 30 seconds, then spoon over the aubergine. Crumble over the feta, then put the remaining oregano sprig between your hands and rub together over the flatbreads so that the dried leaves and flowers rain down on top (or simply scatter).

ENERGY	FAT	SAT FAT	PROTEIN	CARBS	SUGARS	SALT	FIBRE
552kcal	21.1g	5.9g	14.8g	81.2g	5.7g	1.8g	3.1g

WINTER GREENS GNOCCHI
VIVID BLACK CABBAGE & MASCARPONE GORGONZOLA SAUCE

Typically gnocchi is served like a pasta course in Italy, but unconventionally I love serving it like you would a potato side, and this is the most surprising way to celebrate winter's brassica bounty.

SERVES 4 AS A MAIN OR 8 AS A SIDE | TOTAL 20 MINUTES

50g shelled unsalted walnut halves

400g cavolo nero

100g mascarpone cheese

100g Gorgonzola cheese

800g potato gnocchi

Toast the walnuts in a frying pan on a medium heat until golden, then put aside. Tear the stems out of the cavolo nero and discard, then blanch in boiling salted water for 4 minutes. Use tongs to carefully transfer two-thirds of the cavolo straight into a blender, leaving the pan of water on the heat. Remove the remaining cavolo to a board and roughly chop it. Add the mascarpone and most of the Gorgonzola to the blender and blitz until super-smooth, loosening with a splash of cooking water, if needed. Taste and season to perfection with sea salt and black pepper.

Cook the gnocchi in the pan of boiling water for 3 minutes, or until they float to the surface, then drain and toss in the pan with the green sauce and chopped cavolo. Crumble over and fold through most of the walnuts, break over the remaining Gorgonzola and walnuts, then either serve straight away or pop under the grill for a few minutes, until beautifully gratinated.

ENERGY	FAT	SAT FAT	PROTEIN	CARBS	SUGARS	SALT	FIBRE
646kcal	29.4g	13.6g	18.9g	75.2g	3.5g	2.4g	3.4g

ROASTED CAULIFLOWER
CHEAT'S ROMESCO SAUCE & CRUSHED ROASTED ALMONDS

Life is better with romesco sauce in it! Whether you're using it to celebrate beautiful vegetables, like this cauliflower, or eating it with fish, poultry or lamb, it's a joy to make and a pleasure to eat.

SERVES 4 | **TOTAL 45 MINUTES**

1 head of cauliflower (800g)

4 cloves of garlic

100g sourdough bread

50g blanched almonds

1 x 460g jar of roasted red peppers

Preheat the oven to 180°C. Trim away just the tatty outer leaves and the end of the stalk from the cauliflower, then halve, slice into 3cm wedges and sit them in a roasting tray. Toss with a little olive oil, red wine vinegar, sea salt and black pepper, and roast for 35 minutes, or until beautifully golden and tender. Meanwhile, peel the garlic, tear the bread into small chunks, and place on a roasting tray with the almonds. Place in the oven when the cauliflower has just 15 minutes to go.

When the time's up, remove the trays from the oven. Reserve a handful of almonds, then place the rest in a blender with the garlic and toasted bread, drain and add the peppers, 2 tablespoons of olive oil and a swig of red wine vinegar, and whiz until silky-smooth. Loosen with a splash of water, if needed, then taste and season to perfection. Pour on to a serving plate, sit the cauliflower on top, then bash or chop the reserved almonds and sprinkle over, to serve.

ENERGY	FAT	SAT FAT	PROTEIN	CARBS	SUGARS	SALT	FIBRE
286kcal	15.7g	1.9g	11.1g	25.2g	9.8g	0.8g	4.5g

RUMMANIYEH
POMEGRANATE & SMOKY AUBERGINE, GARLIC & LENTIL STEW

This is my version of a popular Palestinian dish. The word 'rumman' translates as pomegranate – this traditionally uses pomegranate molasses, but for ease I've used fresh pomegranate, which I love.

SERVES 4 | **TOTAL 1 HOUR**

2 aubergines (250g each)

4 cloves of garlic

1 tablespoon baharat spice mix

175g dried brown lentils

1 large ripe pomegranate

Quarter the aubergines, then cook for 6 minutes under a hot grill, or until softened and lightly charred, turning regularly. Remove to a board and roughly chop. Peel and finely slice the garlic, place it in a large non-stick frying pan on a medium heat with 1 tablespoon of olive oil and fry until lightly golden, then remove half to a plate for garnish. Add half the chopped aubergine to the pan with the rest of the garlic, along with the spice mix, cook for a few minutes, then add the lentils and 1.5 litres of water. Halve the pomegranate, then, holding one half cut side down in the palm of your hand, bash the back with a spoon so all the seeds tumble out into a bowl and add a good squeeze of juice. Squeeze the rest of the juice into the pan, then simmer on medium for 45 minutes, or until the lentils are tender.

When the time's up, add the rest of the aubergine and most of the pomegranate seeds to the pan, stir well, then taste and season to perfection with sea salt and black pepper. Divide between plates, scatter with the crispy garlic and remaining pomegranate seeds, and finish with a drizzle of extra virgin olive oil, if you like. Delicious served with pitta bread and fresh herbs, if you have any.

ENERGY	FAT	SAT FAT	PROTEIN	CARBS	SUGARS	SALT	FIBRE
200kcal	5.2g	0.8g	12.8g	26.8g	4.8g	0.2g	5.6g

TORTILLA FRITTATA
ROASTED PEPPER, TENDER ONION & POTATO, GOLDEN EGG, WATERCRESS

Inspired by the much-loved Spanish tortilla, this hybrid tortilla frittata is a beautiful gift for any home, and once you've mastered this method, try swapping in peas, artichokes or mushrooms.

SERVES 4 TO 6 | **TOTAL 1 HOUR**

1 onion

1kg potatoes

5 large eggs

½ x 460g jar of roasted red peppers

80g watercress

Peel and very finely slice the onion and potatoes, then toss and mix together. Pour 1cm of olive oil into a 24cm non-stick ovenproof frying pan on a medium heat. After 1 minute, add the potato and onion mix (don't season at this stage, as it will draw the moisture out of the potatoes) and fry gently for 25 minutes, or until tender but mostly without colour, lightly tossing occasionally. Drain the potatoes and onions and leave to cool slightly. Beat the eggs in a bowl, add the cooked potato and onion, then gently fold together and leave for 5 minutes – the potato will start to absorb the egg, and you should see little bubbles surrounding the potato and onion. Drain and finely slice the peppers, then fold into the egg mixture and season to perfection with sea salt and black pepper. Preheat the oven to 160°C.

Quickly wipe out the pan, drizzle in a little olive oil, then place on a low heat. Pour the egg mixture straight into the pan and spread out. Leave for 5 minutes, then bake for 10 minutes. When the time's up, remove from the oven, leave to rest in the pan for 5 minutes, then run a knife around the edge to loosen. Quickly and confidently turn it out, using a plate or flat lid that's bigger than the pan, and serve sprinkled with a little salt and a pinch of watercress. Delicious hot or cold.

ENERGY	FAT	SAT FAT	PROTEIN	CARBS	SUGARS	SALT	FIBRE
791kcal	46.5g	10.6g	44.6g	54g	10.5g	1.2g	7.2g

STUFFED COURGETTES
MINT, FETA & GRAIN FILLING, TOMATO SAUCE

In the Med you cannot escape the love of stuffing veg, which is often misunderstood back at home — the bonus flavour and texture achieved from cooking veg inside veg is really quite remarkable.

SERVES 4 TO 6 | **TOTAL 1 HOUR 10 MINUTES**

8 large courgettes

1 bunch of mint (30g)

2 x 250g packets of cooked mixed grains

100g feta cheese

1 x 400g tin of plum tomatoes

Preheat the oven to 200°C. Trim the courgettes, then slice into 4cm chunks and use an apple corer (or a teaspoon) to hollow them out, leaving a ½cm gap around the edges, reserving the flesh and seeds. Season very generously with sea salt, getting right into the centres (don't worry, we'll rinse it away later). Meanwhile, pick half the mint leaves and finely chop with around 250g of the reserved courgette flesh (discarding the rest), then tip over the grains and break over most of the feta. Season with salt, black pepper and 1 tablespoon of red wine vinegar, then toss and mix together.

Rinse the salt from the courgettes and pat dry, then stuff them with the grain mixture, using your thumbs to really push it in from each side. Line them up in a roasting tray, with one of the cut sides facing down. Roast for 50 minutes, or until beautifully tender. Meanwhile, to make the sauce, scrunch the tomatoes through clean hands into a bowl, add 2 tablespoons of extra virgin olive oil, then finely chop and add the remaining mint leaves, reserving a few baby leaves for garnish. Season to taste with salt, pepper and red wine vinegar. When the time's up, pour the sauce in and around the courgettes and give it 5 further minutes in the oven to warm through. Crumble over the remaining feta, scatter over the baby mint leaves and drizzle with a little extra virgin olive oil, if you like.

ENERGY	FAT	SAT FAT	PROTEIN	CARBS	SUGARS	SALT	FIBRE
469kcal	22.5g	6g	20.1g	47.8g	15.3g	1.8g	9.3g

SQUASH AGRODOLCE
MARINATED OLIVES, PINE NUTS & SEASONAL GREENS

Around the Med you'll see cooking methods that extract the sweetness from veg, and with a swig of vinegar you can achieve a wonderful sweet and sour flavour, taking humble veg to the next level.

SERVES 4 | **TOTAL 55 MINUTES**

1 butternut squash (1.2kg)

2 onions

150g mixed marinated olives

100g pine nuts

500g mixed seasonal greens, such as rainbow chard, cavolo nero

Scrub the squash, then carefully halve lengthways and deseed (I like to leave the skin on because it's nutty and delicious) and peel the onions. Slice and dice everything into 1cm cubes. Place in a large non-stick frying or casserole pan on a medium heat with 2 tablespoons of olive oil and cook for 25 minutes, stirring regularly. Stir in 2 tablespoons of red wine vinegar, then cover and cook for a further 25 minutes, or until sweet and tender. Chop the olives (destone, if needed), plus any of the marinating ingredients, and stir into the pan with the pine nuts. Season to perfection.

Meanwhile, prep the greens, discarding any tough stalks (I like to finely chop any tender stalks and add them to the squash pan). Blanch the greens in a large pan of boiling salted water for 30 seconds, until just tender but still full of life, then drain well and lay out on a clean tea towel. Once cool enough to handle, pile them in the centre, wrap them up, and wring out really well to remove the excess liquid. Roughly chop and divide between plates. Spoon over the squash mixture and serve at your will.

ENERGY	FAT	SAT FAT	PROTEIN	CARBS	SUGARS	SALT	FIBRE
470kcal	32g	3.1g	10.5g	37.1g	20.9g	1.8g	7.8g

PIES & PARCELS

SPINACH & FETA PIE
FRAGRANT DILL & GOLDEN CRUNCHY SESAME SEEDS

Across Greece you'll find wonderful savoury pies bursting with spinach, dill and feta, which inspired me to make this simple 5-ingredient variation. Heavy on the sesame, it's a really beautiful thing.

SERVES 6 | **TOTAL 40 MINUTES**

350g frozen spinach

500g self-raising flour, plus extra for dusting

2 bunches of dill (40g)

200g feta cheese

75g sesame seeds

Preheat the oven to 220°C. Defrost the spinach and squeeze out any excess liquid. Put the flour in a bowl with a pinch of sea salt, then gradually add 325ml of water, mixing with a fork as you go. Once it comes together, use flour-dusted hands to knead until the bowl is clean and the dough is smooth, then transfer to a large oiled surface to rest. Finely chop the dill and spinach (stalks and all), then crumble over the feta and mix well with a pinch of black pepper.

Stretch out the dough on the oiled surface to roughly 40cm x 60cm – I use my hands but you can use a rolling pin, if you prefer. Carefully lift the dough so half of it sits in an oiled 30cm x 40cm tray, with the rest overhanging. Evenly spread the spinach mixture across the dough in the tray, leaving a 2cm gap around the edges. Carefully fold over the overhanging half and press or twist the edges to seal. Rub the top with olive oil, then sprinkle over the sesame seeds, firmly pressing and patting them into the dough. Bake on the bottom shelf of the oven for 25 minutes, or until beautifully golden. Delicious hot, at room temperature or cold from the fridge.

ENERGY	FAT	SAT FAT	PROTEIN	CARBS	SUGARS	SALT	FIBRE
454kcal	15.9g	6.1g	9.3g	59.9g	1.5g	2.3g	4.3g

CRISPY PRAWN PARCELS
DELICATE GOLDEN PASTRY, HARISSA OIL & ZINGY LEMON

My job in this recipe was to make an achievable pastry, similar to the classic brik pastry I tasted in Tunisia, but have struggled to make for years. This is super-fun, just be confident and give it a go.

SERVES 4 (MAKES 12 LITTLE BRIKS) | **TOTAL 45 MINUTES**

250g strong bread flour

400g large raw peeled king prawns

1 large egg

1 lemon

2 tablespoons rose harissa

Pour 150ml of boiling kettle water into a bowl with a large pinch of sea salt. Leave for 2 minutes to cool, then use a fork to mix in the flour until it's dry enough to handle. Knead for 5 minutes, or until smooth and elastic. Rub a 50cm x 50cm clean surface lightly with olive oil. Place the dough on top, cover with the bowl and leave for 10 minutes to relax. Meanwhile, roughly chop half the prawns, and very finely chop the rest. Whisk the egg, and add the prawns. Finely grate in half the lemon zest and season with salt and black pepper. Loosen the harissa with 2 tablespoons of extra virgin olive oil.

Split the dough in half, then gently flatten one piece out as much as possible, leaving the other piece covered. Bit by bit, pull a corner up and gently ease out, stretch and pull it, repeating around 360° of the dough until you have a large, really thin sheet (roughly 40cm x 40cm). Slice the sheet into 6 rough rectangles, and dollop a little harissa in the middle of each. Divide half the prawn mixture between the rectangles, then confidently stretch each corner over the filling to make 6 rustic parcels, embracing their natural shape and patching up as needed. Place a large non-stick frying pan on a medium heat with 1 teaspoon of olive oil, then confidently add the briks (don't worry if any of the filling spills out) and cook for 2½ minutes on each side, or until golden and crispy. Repeat with the remaining dough and filling. Serve with lemon wedges and an extra drizzle of harissa oil, if you like.

ENERGY	FAT	SAT FAT	PROTEIN	CARBS	SUGARS	SALT	FIBRE
440kcal	17.1g	2.6g	26.8g	47.7g	1.4g	1.2g	2.3g

FETA FILO TURNOVERS
FRESH MARJORAM, RUNNY HONEY & PISTACHIO SPRINKLE

When I was a teenager visiting Cyprus on holiday, I was wowed by the recipes that would cook feta rather than just serve it in salads raw. For me, this is so incredibly simple, satisfying and impressive.

SERVES 4 | **TOTAL 20 MINUTES**

4 sheets of filo pastry

200g feta cheese

½ a bunch of marjoram (10g)

25g shelled unsalted pistachios

runny honey, to serve

Lay a sheet of filo on a damp tea towel and brush lightly with olive oil. Crumble a quarter of the feta across one side of the pastry, leaving a 3cm gap around the edges, and pick over a quarter of the marjoram leaves. Carefully fold over the filo, press the edges to seal, then fold in half again, pressing down gently to secure. Brush lightly with olive oil.

Place a large non-stick frying pan on a medium heat with a splash of olive oil, add the filo parcel and cook for 2 minutes on each side, or until golden and crisp, then transfer to a serving plate. Meanwhile, bash or roughly chop the pistachios. Drizzle the parcel with honey and scatter over a quarter of the pistachios. Repeat with the rest of the ingredients, serving each parcel as soon as it's ready.

ENERGY	FAT	SAT FAT	PROTEIN	CARBS	SUGARS	SALT	FIBRE
269kcal	15.6g	9.1g	11.4g	22g	9.2g	1.1g	1.1g

STUFFED CABBAGE LEAVES
SAUSAGE & RICE FILLING, TOMATO SAUCE & OOZY CAMEMBERT

I absolutely love stuffed cabbage dishes but they often have lots of ingredients and stages, so I've really stripped this down with a few shortcuts to make it accessible and achievable in a busy home.

SERVES 4 | TOTAL 1 HOUR

1 large Savoy cabbage

6 spicy pork sausages (400g total)

2 x 250g packets of cooked basmati rice

2 x 400g tins of plum tomatoes

1 x 250g round Camembert cheese

Preheat the oven to 180°C. Trim and click off 8 large cabbage leaves (I like the ones that are slightly yellower – save the rest for another day). Trim off any dry tough stalks and blanch the leaves in a large pan of boiling salted water for 6 minutes, or until bendy and foldable, then drain. Cool under cold running water, then pat dry with a clean tea towel. Meanwhile, remove the sausages from their skins, season with sea salt and black pepper, then scrunch and mix together with the rice. Divide into 8 pieces and squeeze each into a rough cylinder shape.

Open out the cabbage leaves and place a piece of sausage mix in the centre of each. Fold up and roll to create 8 parcels. Scrunch the tomatoes through clean hands into a large shallow casserole pan. Add ½ a tin's worth of water, season to perfection and bring to a simmer on the hob. Carefully arrange the cabbage parcels on top, seam side down. Score around the rim of the Camembert and nestle into the centre, then bake for 30 minutes. Spoon most of the cheese over the cabbage parcels, then bake for a final 10 minutes, or until beautifully golden. To serve, sprinkle with an extra pinch of pepper and drizzle with extra virgin olive oil, if you like. Delicious with crusty bread or mash.

ENERGY	FAT	SAT FAT	PROTEIN	CARBS	SUGARS	SALT	FIBRE
682kcal	39.8g	18g	36.5g	46.7g	10.7g	2.5g	6.3g

STUFFED FOLDED FLATBREAD
MEDITERRANEAN VEG, FRESH MINT, PISTACHIO & TANGY FETA

Inspired by the traditional Turkish flatbreads called pide, this is my stripped-back expression that still packs a flavour punch, and gives you a portable lunch or dinner that can be enjoyed hot or cold.

SERVES 4 | **TOTAL 1 HOUR**

700g frozen chargrilled Mediterranean veg

400g self-raising flour, plus extra for dusting

1 bunch of mint (30g)

30g shelled unsalted pistachios

100g feta cheese

Preheat the oven to 200°C. Tip the frozen veg into a large non-stick frying pan on a medium-high heat with 1 tablespoon of olive oil. Cook for 15 minutes, or until super-soft and sweet, stirring regularly. Meanwhile, put the flour in a bowl with a small pinch of sea salt, then gradually add 275ml of water, mixing with a fork as you go. Tip on to a flour-dusted surface and knead for a few minutes until smooth, then cover and leave to rest.

When the time's almost up on the veg, pick and roughly chop the mint leaves. Bash or chop the pistachios until fine, then mix half into the veg along with most of the mint leaves. Crumble in half the feta and season to perfection. Divide the dough into 4 pieces, then roll each one out to roughly 12cm x 16cm. Spoon a quarter of the filling into the middle of each piece of dough, then pinch and crimp the shortest corners together (like in the picture). Transfer to an oiled baking tray and break over the remaining feta. Brush the dough with olive oil and bake for 20 minutes, or until golden and cooked through. Scatter over the remaining mint leaves and pistachios, to serve.

ENERGY	FAT	SAT FAT	PROTEIN	CARBS	SUGARS	SALT	FIBRE
654kcal	17.9g	6g	20g	104.3g	18.6g	1.5g	11.1g

TRAYBAKED PESTO PIZZA PIE
FRAGRANT ARTICHOKES, SWEET CHERRY TOMATOES & MOZZARELLA

Who doesn't love pizza? There are all sorts of wonderful variations out there and this cheat's dough is a great last-minute go-to for an easy meal. Just a little prep and the oven does the rest for you.

SERVES 4 | **PREP 15 MINUTES** | **COOK 30 MINUTES**

500g self-raising flour, plus extra for dusting

2 tablespoons green pesto

1 x 125g ball of buffalo mozzarella

350g ripe mixed-colour cherry tomatoes

1 x 280g jar of artichoke hearts in oil

Preheat the oven to 200°C. Rub the inside of a 25cm x 35cm baking tray with a little olive oil. Put the flour into a bowl with a small pinch of sea salt, then gradually add 275ml of water, mixing with a fork as you go. Tip on to a flour-dusted surface and knead for a few minutes, until smooth, then use a rolling pin to stretch it out to a large rectangle, just slightly bigger than the tray, dusting the rolling pin with extra flour as you go. Carefully lift the dough into the tray, leaving it overhanging at the edges. Rub the dough all over with pesto, then tear over the mozzarella.

Halve the cherry tomatoes and drain the artichokes, reserving the oil. Drizzle both with 1 tablespoon of artichoke oil, add a pinch of black pepper, then scatter over the dough. Twist and fold in the overhang to make a crust, rubbing the exposed dough with a little more artichoke oil. Cook on the bottom shelf of the oven for 30 minutes, or until golden and puffed up. Great with a salad on the side.

ENERGY	FAT	SAT FAT	PROTEIN	CARBS	SUGARS	SALT	FIBRE
599kcal	17g	5.9g	7.4g	90.9g	2.9g	2.4g	7g

SEAFOOD

OOZY MUSSEL RISOTTO
FRAGRANT FENNEL, SWEET TOMATOES & PARMESAN

Making Italian favourite risotto with just 5 ingredients requires a staunch commitment to big flavour. Juicy mussels are often under-utilized, but they're great value, healthy and a super-sustainable choice.

SERVES 4 | **TOTAL 40 MINUTES**

1 large bulb of fennel, ideally with leafy tops

600g ripe tomatoes

300g risotto rice

1kg mussels, scrubbed, debearded

30g Parmesan cheese, plus extra to serve

Trim the fennel, reserving any leafy tops in a bowl of cold water, then finely chop the rest and place in a large, deep pan on a medium heat with 2 tablespoons of olive oil. Cook for 10 minutes, or until soft, stirring regularly. Meanwhile, slice the tomatoes into sixths and remove the seedy core (to save waste, push the seeds through a coarse sieve to get all of the lovely sweet juices).

Fill and boil the kettle. Add the rice to the pan and stir for 2 minutes. Add a good splash of boiling kettle water and wait until it's been fully absorbed before adding another, stirring constantly and adding more water for 12 minutes. Check the mussels, tap any open ones and if they don't close, discard. Stir the mussels, tomatoes and any juices into the rice, then cover and cook for 7 minutes, or until the mussels have fully opened (discard any that remain closed) and the rice is cooked. Turn the heat off, finely grate and stir in the Parmesan with 2 tablespoons of extra virgin olive oil, and season to perfection. While the rice relaxes for a couple of minutes, I like to remove half the mussels from their shells. Serve sprinkled with the reserved fennel tops and an extra grating of Parmesan, if you like.

ENERGY	FAT	SAT FAT	PROTEIN	CARBS	SUGARS	SALT	FIBRE
559kcal	18.2g	3.8g	21.7g	83.5g	4.7g	1g	8g

PANCETTA PRAWN SKEWERS
JUICY TOMATO SALAD WITH CRISPY GARLIC & ROSEMARY

Celebrating a small handful of ingredients popular across much of southern Europe, this simple salad takes less than 20 minutes to put together. Use ripe in-season tomatoes for the very best flavour.

SERVES 2 | **TOTAL 18 MINUTES**

500g ripe mixed-colour tomatoes

8 large raw shell-on king prawns

4 rashers of smoked pancetta

2 large woody sprigs of rosemary

2 cloves of garlic

Finely slice the tomatoes and arrange nicely on serving plates. Sprinkle with a little sea salt and black pepper, then drizzle with 1 tablespoon of extra virgin olive oil and ½ a tablespoon of red wine vinegar. Peel the prawns, leaving the heads and tails on, then I like to run a small sharp knife down the back of each, discarding the vein, so they butterfly when they cook. Cut each rasher of pancetta in half, and wrap one piece around each prawn. Strip most of the leaves off the rosemary sprigs, then use the stalks to skewer up the prawns (or use wooden skewers). Peel and finely slice the garlic.

Put a large non-stick frying pan on a high heat and, once hot, add the prawns with a little olive oil. Cook for 2 minutes, then flip over and add the rosemary leaves. Cook for a further 2 minutes, or until golden and crisp, adding the garlic for the final minute. Serve everything on top of the tomatoes.

ENERGY	FAT	SAT FAT	PROTEIN	CARBS	SUGARS	SALT	FIBRE
272kcal	12.3g	2.3g	31.6g	9.3g	7.6g	1.6g	3.4g

SIZZLING SQUID
CHORIZO, TOMATO, MINT & LEMON SAUCE

All over the Mediterranean you see really big and bold combinations of surf and turf, and how beautifully it works together – this recipe comes with the harmony of all my favourite ingredients.

SERVES 2 | **TOTAL 16 MINUTES**

2 large super-ripe tomatoes (300g total)

300g whole squid, cleaned, gutted

70g chorizo or spicy sausage

½ a bunch of mint (15g)

1 lemon

Finely grate the tomatoes on a box grater, discarding the skin. Slice into the squid and open it out like a book, lightly score on the inside at ½cm intervals in a criss-cross fashion, slice off and reserve the tentacles, then season with sea salt and black pepper. Slice the chorizo (or break apart if using spicy sausage) and pick the mint leaves. Preheat a large non-stick frying pan on a very high heat. After 3 minutes, drizzle in 1 tablespoon of olive oil, lay the squid in the pan scored side down and use a fish slice to press down on it for 1 minute, then add the tentacles and the chorizo (or spicy sausage). Scatter in half the mint leaves and cook for 3 minutes, tossing regularly.

Remove the scored squid to a plate, then tip the tomatoes into the pan and squeeze in a little lemon juice. Cook for a further 2 minutes, or until thickened and reduced, then divide between plates. Slice the scored squid ½cm thick and scatter over the sauce along with the rest of the mint leaves. Serve with the rest of the lemon cut into wedges, for squeezing over.

ENERGY	FAT	SAT FAT	PROTEIN	CARBS	SUGARS	SALT	FIBRE
344kcal	20.5g	5.8g	32.6g	7.8g	5.1g	1.7g	1.9g

STICKY LEMONY PRAWNS
CHARRED COURGETTES, MIXED GRAINS & PISTACHIOS

The way the Greeks embrace grains inspired me to put this dish together. Celebrating courgettes, lemon and pistachios, as well as beautiful prawns, the interesting way of serving it makes it surprising.

SERVES 2 | **TOTAL 28 MINUTES**

2 courgettes

8 large raw shell-on king prawns

30g shelled unsalted pistachios

2 lemons

1 x 250g packet of cooked mixed grains

Put a large non-stick frying pan on a high heat. Trim and very finely slice the courgettes into rounds and – in batches – lightly char in the hot dry pan in a single layer on one side only, removing to a bowl once done. Meanwhile, peel the prawns, leaving the heads and tails on, then I like to run a small sharp knife down the back of each, discarding the vein, so they butterfly when they cook. Toss with 1 tablespoon of olive oil and season with sea salt and black pepper. Bash or chop the pistachios until fairly fine, then use a speed-peeler to remove strips of peel from one of the lemons.

When all the courgettes are done, add the grains to the bowl with the juice of 1 lemon, 2 tablespoons of extra virgin olive oil and half the pistachios, then season to perfection. Turn the heat down to medium-high, throw in the prawns and lemon peel and fry for 1 minute. Flip the prawns, then tip over the grain mixture and use a spatula to press the grains in and around the prawns. Cook for 3 minutes, then cover with a serving plate that just sits inside the pan and confidently flip out – don't worry if it breaks apart. Scatter over the remaining pistachios and serve with lemon wedges for squeezing over.

ENERGY	FAT	SAT FAT	PROTEIN	CARBS	SUGARS	SALT	FIBRE
548kcal	31.5g	4.6g	21.7g	43.7g	7.4g	1.3g	7.4g

BLACK SQUID

CRISPY OREGANO, GARLIC, BLACK PUDDING & RED WINE

The Spanish love black pudding and seafood combinations – as do I – which has inspired this very quick, deep and delicious stew that really contrasts and elevates the delicate nature of the squid.

SERVES 2 | **TOTAL 16 MINUTES**

300g whole squid, cleaned, gutted

½ a bunch of oregano (10g)

2 cloves of garlic

200g black pudding

200ml red wine

Trim off and reserve the squid tentacles, then slice up the rest, tossing it in a little olive oil and sea salt. Drizzle 1 tablespoon of olive oil into a large non-stick frying pan on a medium-high heat, pick in the oregano and fry until crispy, then remove to a plate. Peel and slice the garlic, add to the pan and fry until lightly golden. Crumble in the black pudding, discarding the skin, then add the squid tentacles and cook for a further 3 minutes, breaking up the black pudding with a spoon as you go. Stir in the wine, allow it to bubble and cook away, then add a good splash of water (to loosen to a ragù consistency) and season to perfection with salt and black pepper. Turn the heat down to medium-low and lay over the sliced squid. Pop the lid on and cook for a final 5 minutes, or until the squid is beautifully tender. Serve sprinkled with the crispy oregano and a drizzle of extra virgin olive oil, if you like.

ENERGY	FAT	SAT FAT	PROTEIN	CARBS	SUGARS	SALT	FIBRE
548kcal	31.8g	9.6g	32.8g	17.7g	0.6g	2.8g	0.4g

EPIC PRAWNS & BEANS
HARISSA & GARLICKY SOURDOUGH CROUTONS

Such a quick and delicious meal – the bright red colour of Tunisian harissa never fails to brighten up a humble jar or tin of beans. To contrast that, simply cooked garlicky prawns and croutons. Wow!

SERVES 2 | **TOTAL 20 MINUTES**

175g sourdough bread

300g large raw peeled king prawns

6 cloves of garlic

½ x 700g jar or 1 x 400g tin of cannellini beans

1 tablespoon harissa or rose harissa

Slice the bread into 2.5cm cubes. Place in a large non-stick frying pan on a high heat and toast until golden, turning regularly. Meanwhile, devein the prawns. Place in a bowl with 1 tablespoon of olive oil and a pinch of sea salt and black pepper, then peel and finely slice the garlic, add to the prawns and toss together. Tip the beans into a saucepan (juices and all), add the harissa, then cover and simmer gently for 5 minutes, or until thickened, stirring occasionally. As soon as the bread is golden, tip the contents of the bowl into the frying pan. Add a splash of red wine vinegar, then cook for 2 minutes, or until the prawns are just cooked, tossing regularly. Taste the beans and season to perfection, then divide between plates. Top with the prawns and crispy croutons, and get stuck in.

ENERGY	FAT	SAT FAT	PROTEIN	CARBS	SUGARS	SALT	FIBRE
431kcal	10.5g	1.6g	40.5g	38.7g	2.2g	1.8g	8.4g

CALAMARI STEW
TOMATOES, PEAS, BEANS & CRÈME FRAÎCHE RIPPLE

I grew up thinking of stews as being mainly meat-based, but in the Mediterranean they have some incredible seafood ones. I've used frozen peas and beans here, but swap in fresh or jarred, if you like.

SERVES 4 | **TOTAL 40 MINUTES**

600g whole squid, cleaned, gutted

4 cloves of garlic

320g frozen bean and pea mix

2 x 400g tins of plum tomatoes

2 tablespoons half-fat crème fraîche

Place the squid in a large non-stick frying pan over a medium heat with 1 tablespoon of olive oil and fry for 3 minutes, turning regularly. Peel and finely slice the garlic, add to the pan and fry for a further 3 minutes, then go in with the frozen beans and peas. Scrunch in the tomatoes through clean hands and give everything a good stir, then cover and stew gently over a low heat for 30 minutes, or until the squid is beautifully tender, stirring occasionally. Remove and slice the squid into chunky pieces, stir it back through the stew and season to perfection with sea salt and black pepper. Ripple through the crème fraîche, then drizzle with a little extra virgin olive oil and serve with crusty bread, if you like.

ENERGY	FAT	SAT FAT	PROTEIN	CARBS	SUGARS	SALT	FIBRE
253kcal	7.9g	1.9g	30.5g	16.3g	8.9g	0.5g	6.5g

PRAWN RICE
VERY SLOW-COOKED ONIONS, SWEET PEPPERS & LEMON

In Catalonia you'll find an abundance of incredible rice dishes before you even see a paella, so I've taken some of the learning from my travels to produce this very delicious, simple dish that people love.

SERVES 4 | **TOTAL 1 HOUR**

4 onions

12 large raw shell-on king prawns

3 mixed-colour peppers

300g paella rice

1 lemon

Boil the kettle. Peel and finely chop the onions, then place in a casserole pan with 2 tablespoons of olive oil on a medium-low heat and cook for 30 minutes, or until dark golden brown, stirring regularly (this base is truly important to the deep delicious flavour – the darker the better). Meanwhile, peel away the shells from 7 of the prawns, then remove the heads (most of the amazing flavour comes from the heads), devein, roughly chop and put aside for later. Place the heads and shells in a small pan with 1 tablespoon of olive oil. Cook for 2 minutes, squashing and turning, to create a delicious prawn oil, then add 1 litre of boiling kettle water and leave to simmer and reduce slightly to make a stock.

Meanwhile, deseed the peppers and dice into 1cm pieces. When the time's up on the onions, add the rice to the pan and cook for 2 minutes. Strain the stock into a large measuring jug, top up with boiling water until you have 800ml, then tip into the rice pan. Cook for 15 minutes with the lid on, stirring in the peppers for the last 5 minutes, then add the chopped prawns, give everything a good stir and season to perfection with sea salt and black pepper. Peel and devein the remaining prawns, leaving the heads and tails on, then arrange nicely on top and use a spatula to press them down into the rice. Cover and cook for a further 5 minutes, then uncover. When you hear the rice start to crackle a little bit, it's time to serve up. Cut the lemon into wedges for squeezing over.

ENERGY	FAT	SAT FAT	PROTEIN	CARBS	SUGARS	SALT	FIBRE
445kcal	8g	1.2g	14.9g	83.6g	16.5g	0.8g	7.6g

CROATIAN MUSSELS
GARLIC BREADCRUMBS, WHITE WINE & TOMATOES

Super-quick and easy, this recipe was inspired by a Croatian seafood dish called buzara, which means stew. I've added tomatoes, which are great mates with wine, herbs and garlicky breadcrumbs.

SERVES 2 | TOTAL 14 MINUTES

50g garlic bread

600g mussels, scrubbed, debearded

1 bunch of flat-leaf parsley (30g)

250g ripe mixed-colour cherry tomatoes

150ml white wine

Whiz the garlic bread into fine breadcrumbs and toast in a large casserole pan on a medium heat, stirring regularly. Meanwhile, check the mussels – if any are open, give them a tap and they should close, if they don't discard them. Finely chop the parsley (stalks and all), and halve the tomatoes. When the breadcrumbs are golden, remove most of them to a plate. Turn the heat up to high, add the mussels, parsley, wine and tomatoes along with 1 tablespoon of olive oil, and cook for 2 minutes. Give it a really good stir, then add 50ml of water and put the lid on for 3 minutes.

When all the mussels have opened and are soft and juicy, they're ready. If any remain closed, discard them. Plate up, drizzle with a little extra virgin olive oil and serve the rest of the crispy breadcrumbs on the side for scattering over.

ENERGY	FAT	SAT FAT	PROTEIN	CARBS	SUGARS	SALT	FIBRE
252kcal	18.6g	4.2g	17g	18.3g	5.1g	1g	2.6g

SEA & MOUNTAIN SKEWERS
PRAWNS, HAM & MUSHROOMS, BURNT LEEKS & CREAMY BEANS

Right the way across the Mediterranean, foods from the sea and mountains collide in truly beautiful ways. And, even more fascinatingly, the friendship between prawns and mushrooms here is divine.

SERVES 2 | **TOTAL 45 MINUTES**

2 medium leeks

8 large raw shell-on king prawns

160g mixed mushrooms

40g Pata Negra or quality Spanish ham

1 x 700g jar of white beans

Preheat the oven to 180°C. Place the whole leeks straight on to the bars of the oven for 40 minutes, or until blackened. Meanwhile, remove the prawn heads, squashing the juices into a small bowl (sounds gross, but trust me!). Peel away the shells, leaving the tails on, then devein and put aside. Place the prawn shells and heads into a small non-stick pan with 4 tablespoons of olive oil. Cook for 10 minutes on a medium heat, squashing and turning regularly, to create a prawn oil, then discard the shells and heads. Meanwhile, finely slice any larger mushrooms and tear the Pata Negra into small pieces (if needed), then carefully divide and thread the prawns, mushrooms and Pata Negra between 4 skewers (I sometimes like to use long woody rosemary sprigs), not packing them too tightly together.

Strip off and discard the outer leaves from the leeks, then finely chop the rest and place in a medium non-stick frying pan with the beans (juices and all) and the reserved prawn juices. Bring to a simmer, then season to perfection with sea salt and 1 tablespoon of red wine vinegar, adding a splash of water to loosen, if needed. Cook the skewers in a large non-stick frying pan on a medium-high heat (or on a barbecue) with a drizzle of olive oil for 5 minutes, or until golden and just cooked through, turning occasionally and lightly pressing down with a fish slice. Spoon the beans on to a warm serving platter, then place the skewers on top and drizzle with the prawn oil, to serve.

ENERGY	FAT	SAT FAT	PROTEIN	CARBS	SUGARS	SALT	FIBRE
589kcal	31.4g	5.5g	36.6g	40.1g	5.3g	1.2g	13.3g

FISH

BREAM & ROASTED GRAPES
CREAMY MUSTARD SAUCE & WILTED BABY SPINACH

Cooking with a Greek chef who specialized in historical regional cooking, I was surprised to see him roast grapes over fire, but the acidity and sweetness is amazing with fish, and this is my expression.

SERVES 2 | TOTAL 25 MINUTES

500g ripe mixed-colour seedless grapes

2 x 300g whole bream, scaled, gutted, gills removed

300g baby spinach

2 tablespoons wholegrain mustard

2 tablespoons crème fraîche

Preheat the oven to 220°C. Pick the grapes into a roasting tray and roast for 5 minutes. When the time's up, nestle in the fish, season from a height with sea salt and black pepper, and drizzle with 1 tablespoon of olive oil. Roast for a further 15 minutes – to check if the fish is cooked, go to the thickest part up near the head – if the flesh flakes easily away from the bone, it's done.

Wilt the spinach in a large non-stick frying pan on a high heat with 1 tablespoon of olive oil, then season to perfection. Place in a colander, squeeze out any excess liquid, then divide between plates. Place the fish on top, and spoon over most of the grapes. Place the tray on the hob over a medium heat and gently squash the remaining grapes with a potato masher. Add the mustard and crème fraîche, mix together and bring to the boil. Taste and adjust the seasoning, add a splash of water to loosen, if needed, then spoon over the fish. Pop an empty plate in the middle of the table for the bones.

ENERGY	FAT	SAT FAT	PROTEIN	CARBS	SUGARS	SALT	FIBRE
496kcal	20.1g	5.3g	38.7g	42.6g	42.4g	1.2g	3.2g

SEARED TUNA SALAD
CHARRED BEANS, FETA-DRESSED POTATOES & OLIVES

Fresh tuna is so delicious and quick to cook. Blistering the green beans is a game-changer. I'm feeling the vibes of a French niçoise salad, but the tangy feta-dressed potatoes nod to the Greek islands.

SERVES 2 | TOTAL 14 MINUTES

220g green beans

10 mixed marinated olives

2 x 150g tuna steaks, ideally 2cm thick

1 x 567g tin of new potatoes

70g feta cheese

Put a large non-stick frying pan on a high heat. Trim the beans and place in the pan until nicely charred, tossing occasionally. Rub ½ a tablespoon of the olive marinade or olive oil over the tuna. Tear up the olives (destone, if needed). Drain and slice the potatoes. Smash up the feta with a splash of its brine in a pestle and mortar or a blender until smooth, adding a splash of water to loosen, if needed. Season with black pepper, toss with the potatoes, then divide between plates.

When the beans are done, toss with the torn olives and a small drizzle each of red wine vinegar and extra virgin olive oil, and scatter over the potatoes. Return the pan to a high heat and sear the tuna for 1 minute on each side, so it's beautifully golden on the outside but blushing pink in the middle. To serve, I like to tear the tuna over the salad, then finish with an extra pinch of pepper.

ENERGY	FAT	SAT FAT	PROTEIN	CARBS	SUGARS	SALT	FIBRE
433kcal	13.1g	5.8g	48.2g	30g	4.1g	1.7g	5.2g

STEAMED FISH AÏOLI
NEW POTATOES, BABY CARROTS & FRESH BASIL

In the south of France they serve a popular dish of boiled seasonal veg and eggs, garlic mayo and salt cod called 'aïoli' (meaning the whole dish, not just the mayo), and this is my 5-ingredient version.

SERVES 4 | **TOTAL 27 MINUTES**

4 x 150g white fish fillets, skin on, scaled, pin-boned

750g new potatoes

500g baby carrots

1 bunch of basil (30g)

4 heaped tablespoons garlic mayo

Season each fish fillet with 1 teaspoon of sea salt (don't worry, we'll rinse it away later) and leave aside. Place the potatoes in a large pan, halving any larger ones, and just cover with boiling salted kettle water. Cook on a medium heat for 10 minutes, then add the carrots. Rinse the fish and pat dry with kitchen paper, then place skin side up in an oiled colander over the pan (making sure the water doesn't come up inside the colander) and cover with a lid. Cook for a further 10 minutes, or until the veg are just tender and the fish is flaky.

Meanwhile, pick the basil leaves into a pestle and mortar, reserving a few pretty ones for garnish, then bash to a paste and muddle in the garlic mayo. To serve, peel away and discard the fish skin, then divide between plates. Drain and divide up the veg, and finish with a good dollop of herby mayo, the reserved basil leaves, a generous pinch of black pepper and a drizzle of extra virgin olive oil, if you like.

ENERGY	FAT	SAT FAT	PROTEIN	CARBS	SUGARS	SALT	FIBRE
389kcal	10.6g	1.4g	32.2g	43.9g	8.8g	1.8g	5.4g

HARISSA SEA BASS
CRISPY ROAST POTATOES, SPEEDY COLOURFUL VEG PICKLE

Inspired by the wonderful pickled veg found in Tunisian markets, the radish and carrot topping packs a huge flavour punch alongside the beautiful harissa-rubbed sea bass and super-crisp potatoes.

SERVES 2 | **TOTAL 1 HOUR**

500g red-skinned or Maris Piper potatoes

2 x 300g whole sea bass, trout or bream, scaled, gutted, trimmed

2 tablespoons rose harissa

160g baby carrots

160g mixed-colour radishes, ideally with leaves

Preheat the oven to 200°C. Peel the potatoes, cut into 1cm-thick slices, then toss with 1 tablespoon of olive oil and a pinch of sea salt and black pepper. Place in a large roasting tray, then transfer to the oven for 20 minutes. Meanwhile, slice a criss-cross pattern into both sides of the fish at 2cm intervals, then rub all over with half the harissa. When the time's up on the potatoes, turn them over, then nestle in the fish and cook for a further 20 minutes, or until the fish is just cooked through.

Scrub and trim the carrots and radishes, then slice at an angle, ½cm thick (use a crinkle-cut knife, if you've got one), keeping the radish leaves if fresh, small and tasty. Place in a bowl, season generously with salt and pepper, then add 1 tablespoon of extra virgin olive oil, 2 tablespoons of red wine vinegar and the remaining harissa, and toss together. Serve the fish topped with potatoes and pickled veg.

ENERGY	FAT	SAT FAT	PROTEIN	CARBS	SUGARS	SALT	FIBRE
520kcal	21.1g	2.1g	32.6g	52.4g	7.6g	1.8g	6.4g

LIME-CURED SEA BASS
JUICY PEACH, FISH CRACKLING, TARRAGON & FRESH CHILLI

Inspired by a group of wonderful French chefs who sailed me out to a little island just off Marseille and cured some fresh fish with citrus and herbs, this is my expression of that summery delight.

SERVES 4 AS A STARTER | **TOTAL 15 MINUTES**

2 x 150g super-fresh white fish fillets, such as sea bass or bream, skin off and reserved, pin-boned

4 limes

1 ripe peach

½ a bunch of tarragon (10g)

1–2 mixed-colour chillies

Get your fishmonger to fillet the freshest white fish, remove the skin for you to keep, and slice the boneless white fish into 1cm chunks. Place a non-stick frying pan on a medium heat with a drizzle of olive oil, add the fish skin and fry for 3 minutes, or until crisp, turning halfway, then remove to a plate.

Finely grate the zest of 1 lime and put aside, then squeeze the juice from all 4 into a shallow bowl and season with a generous pinch of sea salt and black pepper. Stir in the white fish and it will begin to cure. Destone and very finely slice the peach, pick the tarragon leaves and finely slice the chilli(es), then gently toss them all into the bowl. To serve, crack over the crispy fish skin and scatter over the reserved lime zest, then finish with a drizzle of extra virgin olive oil, if you like.

ENERGY	FAT	SAT FAT	PROTEIN	CARBS	SUGARS	SALT	FIBRE
166kcal	9.3g	1.9g	15.7g	5.5g	4.7g	0.6g	0.8g

QUICK SALT COD
CRISPY POTATOES, SILKY EGGS, PARSLEY & OLIVE TAPENADE

Although Portugal doesn't have a coastline in the Med, they're included, and this take on fish and chips, inspired by bacalhau à Brás, is my stripped-back version of their much-loved comfort food dish.

SERVES 2 | **TOTAL 30 MINUTES**

2 x 150g cod fillets, skin on, scaled, pin-boned

500g Maris Piper potatoes

2 large eggs

½ a bunch of flat-leaf parsley (15g)

2 teaspoons black olive tapenade

Season the cod very generously all over with sea salt (don't worry, we'll rinse it away later) and leave aside. Meanwhile, scrub and chop the potatoes into 1cm cubes, then place in a large non-stick frying pan on a medium heat with 2 tablespoons of olive oil and a pinch of salt and black pepper. Cook for 10 minutes, or until slightly golden, tossing occasionally.

Rinse the fish and pat dry with kitchen paper (this fast salting will season the fish, but most importantly will make it flakier and juicier). Push the potatoes to one side of the pan, then add the fish and cook for 3½ minutes on each side, or until just cooked, not forgetting to take care of the potatoes. Meanwhile, beat the eggs together in a bowl. Pick half the parsley leaves and put aside, then finely chop the rest (stalks and all) and add to the eggs. Remove the pan from the heat, transfer the fish to a plate, then pour the egg mixture over the crispy potatoes in the pan. Toss vigorously together for 30 seconds (the residual heat of the pan will just cook the eggs to a silky-soft scramble), then divide between serving plates. Remove and discard the fish skin, and flake the flesh over the potatoes, then dot over the olive tapenade. Scatter with the remaining parsley leaves, dressed with a little extra virgin olive oil and red wine vinegar. Delicious served with a fresh green salad.

ENERGY	FAT	SAT FAT	PROTEIN	CARBS	SUGARS	SALT	FIBRE
377kcal	16.2g	2.9g	37.4g	22g	1.1g	1.8g	2.2g

WHITE FISH STEW
SILKY SLOW-COOKED LEEK & LEMON SAUCE

This unassuming-looking dish is an incredibly delicious way to cook and serve fish, using the classic Greek technique of turning the cooking broth into a silky sauce using the liaison of eggs and lemon.

SERVES 4 | **TOTAL 32 MINUTES**

2 large leeks

4 x 150g white fish fillets, skin on, scaled, pin-boned, ideally 2cm thick

2 tablespoons plain flour

1 lemon

2 large eggs

Wash, trim and very finely slice the leeks, then place in a large casserole pan on a low heat with 1 tablespoon of olive oil and 200ml of water. Season with sea salt and black pepper, then cover and cook gently for 20 minutes, or until soft and sweet, stirring occasionally. When the time's almost up, place a large non-stick frying pan on a high heat with 2 tablespoons of olive oil. Coat the fish fillets with flour, cook for 2 minutes on each side, then transfer them to the casserole pan, nestling them into the leeks. Pour in 250ml of boiling water, cover with a lid and cook on a medium heat for 4 minutes.

Meanwhile, finely grate the lemon zest and put aside, and squeeze the juice into a bowl. Separate the eggs (save the whites for making meringues another day), add the yolks to the lemon juice with a pinch of salt, and beat together well. Remove the lid from the pan, spoon a good splash of the hot liquid into the egg mixture, and keep whisking. Take the pan off the heat and pour in the contents of the bowl. Constantly jiggling the pan and using a spatula, keep the mixture moving around the fish for a couple of minutes. Pop the lid back on, keep jiggling the pan for a further 2 minutes, or until beautifully silky and thickened, then season with a pinch of pepper. Serve with a drizzle of extra virgin olive oil and with the reserved lemon zest scattered over.

ENERGY	FAT	SAT FAT	PROTEIN	CARBS	SUGARS	SALT	FIBRE
300kcal	14.4g	2.5g	33.1g	10.1g	1.9g	1.3g	0.4g

SIMPLE STEAMED FISH
SWEET PEPPERS & LEEKS, HERBY ORANGE DRESSING

Inspired by flavours that will transport you to the Greek coast, this delicate dish simply celebrates white fish fillets. Easy to halve if you're serving two, you'll be glad to have this one up your sleeve.

SERVES 4 | **TOTAL 32 MINUTES**

4 x 150g white fish fillets, skin off, pin-boned

3 mixed-colour peppers

1 large leek

½ a bunch of oregano (10g)

1 large juicy orange

To amplify the flakiness, very generously dust the fish with sea salt (don't worry, we'll rinse it away later) and leave aside. Put a large shallow casserole pan on a medium heat. Chop the peppers into 2cm chunks, discarding the seeds and stalks, adding them to the pan as you go with 2 tablespoons of olive oil. Quarter the leek lengthways and wash, then slice 2cm thick. Add to the pan, season with salt and black pepper, and cook for 15 minutes, or until sweet and lightly golden, stirring regularly and adding splashes of water, if needed. Strip the oregano leaves into a pestle and mortar with a pinch of salt and pound into a paste. Squeeze in half the orange juice, then add 1 tablespoon of red wine vinegar and 2 tablespoons of extra virgin olive oil and muddle together.

Rinse the fish and pat dry with kitchen paper. Nestle the fish into the veg, squeeze in the remaining orange juice and add 100ml of water, then cover the pan, reduce the heat to low and cook for 7 minutes, or until the fish is just cooked. Drizzle the orange dressing over the fish and veg and serve.

ENERGY	FAT	SAT FAT	PROTEIN	CARBS	SUGARS	SALT	FIBRE
276kcal	14.5g	2.1g	29.1g	7.6g	7g	1.3g	2.6g

ELEGANT FISH CARPACCIO
FRESH BREAM, GREEN CHILLI, ZINGY LIME, GRAPES & ROCKET

We all need a great fishmonger in our lives, whether it's a shop, market, van or online. Eating raw fish is not rocket science, it's incredibly easy, healthy and delicious, but it needs to be super-fresh.

SERVES 2 AS A MAIN OR 4 AS A STARTER | TOTAL 15 MINUTES

2 limes

10 mixed-colour seedless grapes

½ a fresh green chilli

2 x 150g super-fresh bream fillets, skin off, pin-boned

20g rocket

Squeeze the lime juice into a bowl and season with a couple of good pinches of sea salt. Finely slice the grapes and chilli, add to the bowl and toss together. Slice the fish at an angle into 1cm pieces and gently bash between two sheets of greaseproof paper with a rolling pin until roughly 2mm thick – you'll need to work in batches. Peel the fish from the paper and arrange nicely over two serving plates or one big platter. Spoon over the grapes and chilli, drizzling with the seasoned lime juice. Scatter over the rocket, then drizzle with 1 tablespoon of extra virgin olive oil. Delicious served as is, but some people like something crunchy, like a cracker or toasted bread with it – whatever makes you happy.

ENERGY	FAT	SAT FAT	PROTEIN	CARBS	SUGARS	SALT	FIBRE
219kcal	10.9g	0.9g	26.9g	3.5g	3.5g	1.4g	0.4g

CRISPY-SKINNED MACKEREL
POMEGRANATE SEEDS & SYRUP, RAS EL HANOUT & WALNUTS

Across the Mediterranean, you see fish and fruit coming together in wonderful ways. Pomegranates, which are prolific, give you sweetness and sourness, which is perfect to cut through the oily fish.

SERVES 2 | TOTAL 25 MINUTES

150g Greek yoghurt

2 x 200g whole mackerel, gutted, pin-boned, butterflied

2 heaped teaspoons ras el hanout, plus extra to serve

1 large ripe pomegranate

20g shelled unsalted walnut halves

Line a sieve with a few pieces of kitchen paper, tip in the yoghurt, then pull up the paper and very gently apply pressure so that the liquid starts to drip through into a bowl. Leave in the fridge to drain. Open out each mackerel and coat heavily all over with ras el hanout and a pinch of sea salt and black pepper. Place skin side down in a large non-stick frying pan on a medium heat with 2 tablespoons of olive oil for 7 minutes, covering with a lid for the first 4 minutes, and basting once uncovered, then remove to serving plates, skin side up. Meanwhile, halve the pomegranate and, holding one half cut side down in your fingers, bash the back of it with a spoon so all the seeds tumble into a bowl. Squeeze the juice into another bowl and pour into the hot pan to reduce down to a syrup.

Season the hung yoghurt to perfection, then spoon over the crispy fish. Drizzle over the pomegranate syrup and top with a few pomegranate seeds (saving the rest for another day). Sprinkle lightly with ras el hanout and crumble over the walnuts, then drizzle with extra virgin olive oil, to finish.

ENERGY	FAT	SAT FAT	PROTEIN	CARBS	SUGARS	SALT	FIBRE
524kcal	44.1g	10.7g	22.4g	9g	8.4g	1.2g	0.9g

CHICKEN & DUCK

POT-ROAST CHICKEN
FONDANT POTATOES, HERBY SALSA, ROASTED GARLIC

Herby salsas are much loved in Catalan cooking, so, inspired by a recent trip to Barcelona, I've embellished this chicken and these rich, stock-cooked potatoes with a vibrant nutty number.

SERVES 4 | **TOTAL 1 HOUR 35 MINUTES**

1 x 1.5kg whole chicken

1kg potatoes

1 bunch of flat-leaf parsley (30g)

1 bulb of garlic

40g blanched hazelnuts

Preheat the oven to 180°C. Rub the chicken all over with olive oil, sea salt and black pepper, then brown in a large casserole pan on a high heat, removing it to a plate once golden all over (roughly 5 minutes). Meanwhile, peel the potatoes and chop into 5cm chunks. Pour 700ml of water into the pan, then add the parsley stalks, garlic bulb (reserving 1 garlic clove for later) and the potatoes. Bring to the boil on the hob for 15 minutes, season lightly, then pop the chicken on top and place in the oven for 1 hour 15 minutes, or until the chicken is golden and cooked through.

Meanwhile, peel and finely chop the reserved garlic clove, very finely chop the parsley leaves, and roughly chop the hazelnuts. Decant into a small serving bowl, stir in 3 tablespoons of extra virgin olive oil and 4 tablespoons of water, and season to perfection. Transfer the chicken and potatoes to a serving platter, spoon over the herby salsa and serve the garlic bulb on the side, for squeezing over.

ENERGY	FAT	SAT FAT	PROTEIN	CARBS	SUGARS	SALT	FIBRE
669kcal	27.2g	5.6g	62.9g	45.7g	2g	1.1g	4g

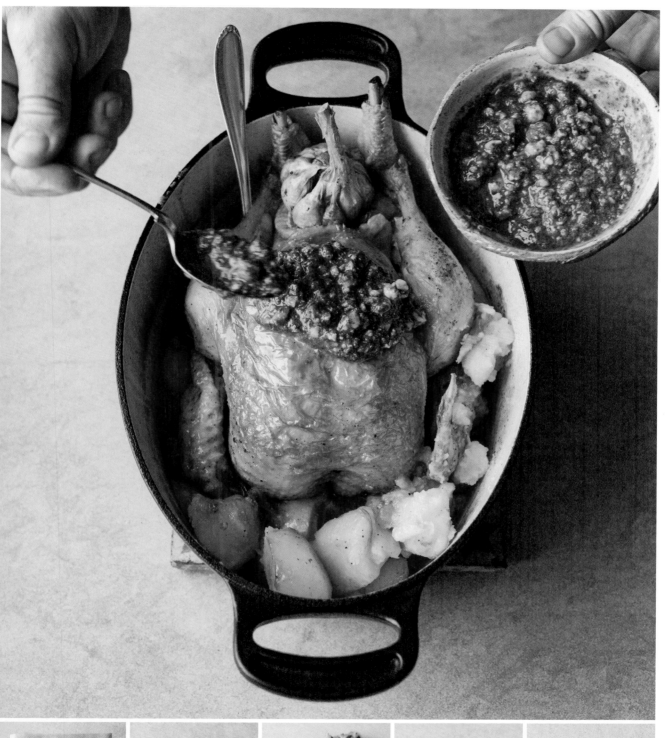

BAHARAT CHICKEN SHISH
SPICED YOGHURT MARINADE, LEMON & ROASTED GARLIC

Inspired by the Turkish shish, this is a very simple, delicious kebab that anyone can make, using a blend of fragrant spices. I love the contrast between the crispy outside and the juicy tender inside.

SERVES 4 | **TOTAL 55 MINUTES, PLUS MARINATING**

6 skinless, boneless chicken thighs

4 tablespoons natural yoghurt

2 teaspoons baharat spice mix, plus extra to serve

2 lemons

1 bulb of garlic

Place the chicken thighs in a bowl with the yoghurt, spice mix, 1 tablespoon of olive oil and a pinch of sea salt and black pepper. Slice 6 thin slices off one of the lemons and put aside, then squeeze the juice from the rest of the lemon into the bowl. Toss everything together really well, then cover and leave to marinate in the fridge for at least 2 hours, preferably overnight.

Preheat the oven to 200°C. Thread the chicken and lemon slices evenly on to one large metal skewer, like you see in the picture, and rest it over a roasting tray that's slightly smaller than the skewer (so that the meat is suspended above the tray). Slice the garlic bulb in half and place cut side down in the tray. Halve and throw in the remaining lemon, then roast for 40 minutes, or until gnarly and cooked through. To serve, slice the chicken off the skewer, squeeze the sweet roasted garlic out of its papery skins and toss with the chicken, and sprinkle over a little extra baharat spice. Drizzle over any tray juices, and serve the jammy lemon alongside, for squeezing over. Delicious served with flatbreads, salad and pickles.

ENERGY	FAT	SAT FAT	PROTEIN	CARBS	SUGARS	SALT	FIBRE
278kcal	15g	4g	31.7g	3.8g	1.8g	1g	1.2g

CRISPY PAPRIKA CHICKEN
SWEET RAINBOW PEPPERS, POTATOES & FRAGRANT THYME

Roasting chicken directly on the oven bars means you get super-crispy skin and all the tasty juices rain down on to the lucky veg below. Spanish favourite paprika gives you big flavour all round.

SERVES 4 | **TOTAL 1 HOUR**

1kg potatoes

3 mixed-colour peppers

1 x 1.5kg whole chicken

1 heaped tablespoon smoked paprika

1 bunch of thyme (20g)

Preheat the oven to 200°C. Scrub the potatoes and chop into 3cm chunks. Chop the peppers roughly the same size, removing the seeds and stalks. Place it all in a large roasting tray and toss with 1 tablespoon of olive oil and a little sea salt and black pepper. Using a large sharp knife, carefully cut the chicken in half. Drizzle with 1 tablespoon each of olive oil and red wine vinegar, then rub all over with the paprika and a pinch of salt and pepper. Put the tray of veg on the bottom shelf of the oven, sit the chicken halves skin side up directly on the oven shelf above, then roast for 40 minutes.

When the time's up, rub the thyme with a drizzle of olive oil. Pull out the tray of veg, give it a good shake, then strip and scatter over half the thyme. Lay the rest of the thyme sprigs on top of the chicken and roast for a final 5 minutes, or until everything is beautifully cooked through, then serve.

ENERGY	FAT	SAT FAT	PROTEIN	CARBS	SUGARS	SALT	FIBRE
652kcal	23.6g	5.4g	62.8g	40.2g	6.6g	1.1g	5.8g

ROAST DUCK WITH GRAPES
GROUND CLOVES, CARAMELIZED ONIONS & ROSEMARY

I was enchanted by the grilling, roasting and serving of fresh grapes with rich meat or fish dishes I saw on some of the Greek islands. It works incredibly well – naturally sweet and sour. So delicious!

SERVES 6 | **TOTAL 2 HOURS 20 MINUTES**

1 x 2kg whole duck, giblets reserved

1 tablespoon ground cloves

4 red onions

1 bunch of rosemary (20g)

500g mixed-colour seedless grapes

Preheat the oven to 180°C. In a large roasting tray, rub the duck and neck (reserve the livers, kidneys and heart) all over with 1 tablespoon of olive oil, the cloves and a really good pinch of sea salt and black pepper. Peel and quarter the onions, throw them into the tray with the neck and toss together, then add 2 tablespoons of water and sit the duck on top. Stuff half the rosemary into the cavity, then roast for 1 hour 30 minutes. Remove from the oven, skim off most of the fat (reserve it in a jam jar) and baste the duck with the pan juices. Pick in the grapes, then roast for a further 30 minutes, or until the duck legs are tender. Remove the duck to a serving platter and spoon half the grapes and onions into a bowl. Place the tray over a medium heat, pour in 500ml of boiling kettle water, and simmer for 5 minutes, mashing the grapes and scraping up any sticky goodness from the bottom of the pan.

Meanwhile, chop the livers, kidneys and heart into 1cm dice. Drizzle a good splash of the duck fat into a non-stick saucepan over a medium heat. Pick in the remaining rosemary leaves, leave to sizzle until crisp, then remove to kitchen paper. Add the chopped giblets and toss over the heat for 3 minutes, or until cooked through. Pass the contents of the tray through a coarse sieve into the pan and season to taste. Add the reserved grapes and onions, toss together over a low heat, then spoon over the duck and sprinkle with rosemary. Pour the gravy into a jug and serve alongside.

ENERGY	FAT	SAT FAT	PROTEIN	CARBS	SUGARS	SALT	FIBRE
244kcal	9g	2.4g	20.2g	22.6g	20g	0.6g	4g

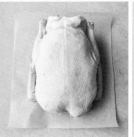

GARLIC CHICKEN
CREAMY CHICKPEAS, SPINACH & SUMAC

Inspired by some of the wonderful flavours of Lebanon, this quick dish is perfect for an easy meal. Hunting out nice fat jarred chickpeas is game-changing when it comes to both flavour and texture.

SERVES 2 | **TOTAL 18 MINUTES**

4 cloves of garlic

2 x 150g skinless chicken breasts

½ x 700g jar of chickpeas

250g baby spinach

1 heaped teaspoon sumac

Peel the garlic cloves and slice lengthways, then place in a large non-stick frying pan on a high heat with 1 tablespoon of olive oil, stirring regularly. Slice each chicken breast lengthways into 3 strips, then toss with a pinch of sea salt and black pepper. Once the garlic is nicely golden, quickly remove from the pan with a slotted spoon, leaving the flavoured oil behind. Go in with the chicken and cook for 5 minutes, or until golden and cooked through, turning regularly.

Remove the chicken from the pan and tip in the chickpeas (juices and all). Add the spinach, along with most of the garlic and 1 tablespoon of red wine vinegar, then toss over the heat until the spinach has wilted and the chickpeas are hot through. Season to perfection with salt and pepper, then return the chicken to the pan and finish with the reserved garlic and a generous dusting of sumac.

ENERGY	FAT	SAT FAT	PROTEIN	CARBS	SUGARS	SALT	FIBRE
406kcal	13.3g	2.2g	48.8g	23.2g	3.1g	1.3g	1.1g

LEMON-TZATZIKI CHICKEN
FLUFFY PAN-JUICE RICE, JAMMY ONIONS & ROASTED LEMONS

A brilliant Greek-inspired one-pan family dish. Tzatziki makes a fantastic ready-to-go marinade — it's untraditional used like this, but I can totally vouch for its deliciousness and ability to tenderize meat.

SERVES 4 | **TOTAL 2 HOURS, PLUS MARINATING**

1 x 1.5kg whole chicken

2 x 200g tubs of tzatziki

2 lemons

4 mixed-colour onions

300g basmati rice

Use a sharp knife to carefully cut down the back of the chicken, so you can open it out flat. Rub half the tzatziki all over the chicken with the juice of ½ a lemon and good pinch of sea salt and black pepper, then cover and leave to marinate in the fridge for at least 2 hours, preferably overnight. Preheat the oven to 180°C. Peel the onions, then very finely chop half an onion and place in a bowl with the juice of ½ a lemon and a pinch of salt to make a pickle. Quarter the rest of the onions and place in a deep tray or ovenproof pan, then halve and add the remaining lemon. Place the chicken skin side up on top (it should fit snugly) and drizzle with ½ a tablespoon of olive oil. Roast for 1 hour 10 minutes, or until beautifully golden and the leg meat pulls easily away from the bone.

When the time's up, remove the chicken with half the roasted onions and one jammy lemon half to a board for later. Using tongs, carefully squeeze the other jammy lemon half into the pan of tray juices, then cut off and discard the white pith and finely slice the skin, along with the rest of the onions. Put them back into the pan or tray along with the rice and 600ml of boiling salted water, then cover and cook on the hob on a medium-low heat for 12 minutes, or until tender. Spoon the rice into a serving dish, place the chicken, any resting juices and the reserved roasted onions on top, and spoon over the remaining tzatziki. Drizzle with 1 tablespoon of extra virgin olive oil and serve with the pickle and the reserved cooked lemon half, for squeezing over.

ENERGY	FAT	SAT FAT	PROTEIN	CARBS	SUGARS	SALT	FIBRE
682kcal	15.6g	5.8g	61.4g	79g	13g	2.4g	5g

CHICKEN & MERGUEZ STEW
BEAUTIFUL BAY MARINADE, SLOW-COOKED ONIONS & BEANS

This is a really delicious Tunisian-style casserole, using the French cassoulet as inspiration to create massive flavour with hardly any ingredients. Feel free to add a little harissa into the mix, if you like.

SERVES 4 | **TOTAL 1 HOUR**

4 onions

5 Merguez sausages (300g)

1 x 1.2kg whole chicken

12 fresh bay leaves

2 x 400g tins of mixed beans

Peel, halve and roughly slice the onions, then place in a large casserole pan on a medium heat with 1 tablespoon of olive oil. Squeeze the meat from 1 of the sausages into the pan and fry for 20 minutes, stirring regularly and breaking up the sausage. Meanwhile, carefully cut up the chicken (you'll need to split the legs into thighs and drumsticks and remove the wings), and cut the breast into quarters (on the bone) – have a go at this yourself, or ask your butcher to do it for you.

Remove the stalks from 8 of the bay leaves, bash the leaves to a mush with a pinch of sea salt in a pestle and mortar, then muddle in 1 tablespoon each of extra virgin olive oil and red wine vinegar. Rub half of the marinade all over the chicken, getting into all the nooks and crannies. Put a large non-stick frying pan on a medium-high heat with 1 tablespoon of olive oil, and brown the remaining sausages with the thighs, drumsticks and wings, transferring them to the casserole pan when beautifully golden. Brown the breast skin side down for 3 minutes, then transfer to the casserole pan. Meanwhile, drain one of the tins of beans, then tip both tins into the casserole pan with the rest of the bay leaves. Gently mix together, then turn the heat down to medium-low and cook for 30 minutes with the lid on, or until beautifully tender. Drizzle over the rest of the bay marinade, to serve.

ENERGY	FAT	SAT FAT	PROTEIN	CARBS	SUGARS	SALT	FIBRE
644kcal	23.6g	6.9g	69.4g	39.1g	14.3g	2g	10.7g

ZA'ATAR CHICKEN
BAKED IN A CRUST WITH LEMON & STICKY ONIONS

Using a simple flour and water dough that bakes into a crust ensures you get incredibly juicy meat, every time. Za'atar, a beautiful herby spice mix from the Levantine coast, provides big flavour here.

SERVES 4 | **TOTAL 1 HOUR 40 MINUTES**

2 tablespoons za'atar

1 x 1.5kg whole chicken

4 onions

1 lemon

500g plain flour, plus extra for dusting

Preheat the oven to 180°C. Mix the za'atar with a pinch of sea salt and black pepper and 2 tablespoons of olive oil, then rub all over the chicken, getting into all the nooks and crannies. Place the chicken in a snug-fitting casserole pan on a high heat, turning with tongs for 15 minutes, or until golden all over. Meanwhile, peel and quarter the onions, stab the lemon all over with a fork, then quarter lengthways. Put the flour into a bowl and gradually mix in 300ml of water with a fork until you have a dough. Knead until smooth, then roll out on a flour-dusted surface until a little bigger than the pan.

Lift up the chicken and place the onions underneath with 2 tablespoons of red wine vinegar. Sit the chicken back on top and nestle the lemon wedges around it, sitting some wedges in the cavity and on the wings so they don't pierce the dough. Remove the pan from the heat and lay the dough over the top, carefully pinching it at the edges to seal. Place in the oven for 1 hour 10 minutes, then crack open and discard the crust. Baste the chicken with the juices, then serve with rice, couscous or flatbreads.

ENERGY	FAT	SAT FAT	PROTEIN	CARBS	SUGARS	SALT	FIBRE
488kcal	21.8g	5g	58.4g	14.8g	11.4g	1.4g	4.8g

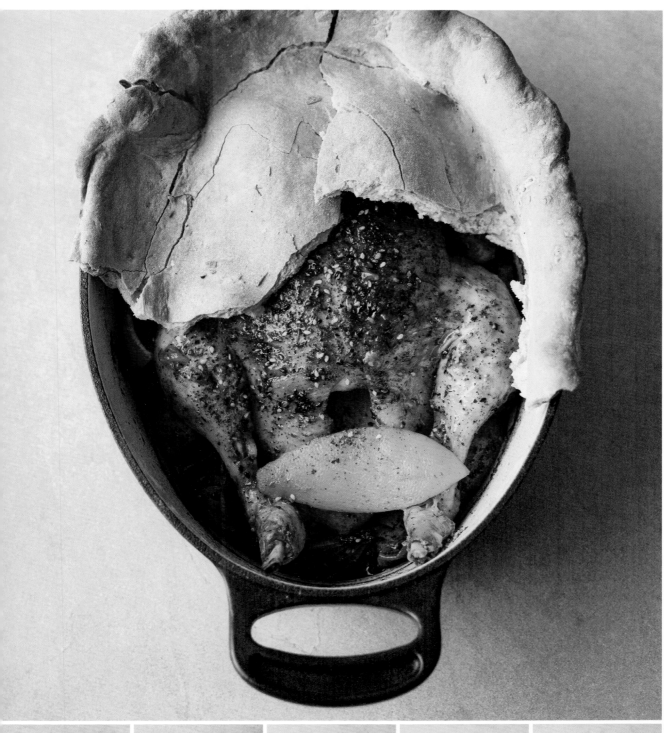

COUSCOUS & CHICKEN BAKE
TZATZIKI MARINADE, SWEET RED PEPPERS & CHARRED ONION

Couscous is used across the Mediterranean in so many wonderful ways — here I'm putting it centre stage to create the most outrageous bake, with a crispy outside and beautifully fluffy centre.

SERVES 4 | **TOTAL 1 HOUR 15 MINUTES, PLUS MARINATING**

1 x 460g jar of roasted red peppers

2 x 200g tubs of tzatziki

1kg mixed chicken thighs and drumsticks, skin on, bone in

4 red onions

300g couscous

Preheat the oven to 180°C. Whiz one of the jarred peppers in a blender with 1 tub of tzatziki and a pinch of sea salt and black pepper. Pour over the chicken and leave to marinate for at least 2 hours, preferably overnight. Peel and quarter the onions, place them in a 28cm non-stick ovenproof frying pan with 1 tablespoon of olive oil on a medium heat for 10 minutes, or until dark and gnarly, turning regularly, then remove to a plate. Drizzle 1 tablespoon of olive oil into the pan, then add the marinated chicken and brown for 10 minutes, turning regularly. Place the onions back in the pan, tear in the remaining peppers, then roast in the oven for 25 minutes.

Meanwhile, in a bowl, just cover the couscous with boiling kettle water, season with salt and pepper, and cover. Leave to hydrate for 3 minutes, then fluff up with a fork. When the time's up, remove the pan from the oven, tip over the couscous and carefully pat down to compress. Roast for 10 minutes, then confidently and carefully turn out on to a large plate or platter and top with dollops of the remaining tzatziki. Serve straight from the oven and let everyone dig in.

ENERGY	FAT	SAT FAT	PROTEIN	CARBS	SUGARS	SALT	FIBRE
790kcal	30.2g	9.8g	53.2g	81g	19.2g	2.3g	8.3g

CHICKPEA CHICKEN
FENNEL MARINADE, SUPER-JUICY TOMATO SALAD

In the south of France I really enjoyed eating the chickpea-flour chips called 'panisse', and I've used them as inspiration for this chickpea and roast chicken salad, with lovely texture and epic flavour.

SERVES 4 | **TOTAL 1 HOUR 20 MINUTES**

3 x 400g tins of chickpeas

1 tablespoon fennel seeds

1 x 1.5kg whole chicken

500g mixed-colour tomatoes

180g mixed salad leaves

Preheat the oven to 180°C. Drain the chickpeas really well, then tip into a food processor and pulse with a good pinch of sea salt and black pepper, keeping a bit of texture. Line a large baking tray with greaseproof paper and spread half the chickpea mixture in the centre, flattening it down slightly. Squash and scrunch little handfuls of the remaining mixture and dot around the edges of the tray (think golf-ball sized), then place the tray at the bottom of the oven. Bash the fennel seeds in a pestle and mortar with a good pinch of salt and pepper, then muddle in 1 tablespoon each of olive oil and red wine vinegar. Carefully cut down the back of the chicken to open it out, then rub the marinade all over. Place directly on the bars of the oven, above the tray of chickpeas, and roast for 1 hour, or until beautifully golden and cooked through, turning the tray of chickpeas halfway – you'll end up with a mixture of crispy and wonderfully stodgy chickpeas, flavoured with delicious chicken juices.

Finely chop the tomatoes, toss them in a bowl with the salad leaves and 1 tablespoon of extra virgin olive oil, and season to perfection. Portion up the chicken and serve with the chickpeas and salad.

ENERGY	FAT	SAT FAT	PROTEIN	CARBS	SUGARS	SALT	FIBRE
628kcal	25.1g	5.7g	70.1g	31.1g	4.6g	1g	10.5g

SUMAC CHICKEN
ROASTED FLATBREADS, DARK & STICKY ONIONS, PINE NUTS

A Palestinian-style spiced chicken flatbread, much-loved and cooked all year round, but especially during the olive oil harvest – the flavour of each ingredient really shines in this comforting meal.

SERVES 4 | **TOTAL 1 HOUR 20 MINUTES**

6 red onions

1kg mixed chicken thighs and drumsticks, skin on, bone in

1 heaped tablespoon sumac, plus extra to serve

50g pine nuts

4 flatbreads

Preheat the oven to 170°C. Peel the onions and slice ½cm thick, then place in a large roasting tray with the chicken, a good pinch of sea salt and black pepper, 1 tablespoon each of red wine vinegar and olive oil, and the sumac. Toss to coat, arranging the chicken skin side up in a single layer. Roast for 1 hour, or until the chicken is cooked through, giving the tray a good shake and adding 100ml of water halfway. With 10 minutes to go, add the pine nuts, then remove from the oven.

Place the flatbreads directly on the bars of the oven until beautifully golden, and shred the chicken apart with forks, discarding any bones. Divide and spoon the sticky onions over the warm flatbreads, taking them right to the edges, then scatter over the chicken and finish with extra sumac, if you like. Delicious with dollops of yoghurt or a seasonal green salad on the side.

ENERGY	FAT	SAT FAT	PROTEIN	CARBS	SUGARS	SALT	FIBRE
567kcal	28.7g	6g	44.7g	32.9g	11.2g	1.1g	4.8g

QUICK CRISPY DUCK
CREAMY WHITE BEANS, CHARRED BROCCOLI, ORANGE & SAGE

Celebrating some classic French ingredients, this exciting dish is about big flavour and texture, but minimum work. Plus, it's on the table in only 20 minutes, making it a perfect midweek dinner for two.

SERVES 2 | **TOTAL 22 MINUTES**

2 x 150g duck breast fillets, skin on

2 sprigs of sage

200g purple sprouting broccoli

1 large juicy orange

1 x 400g tin of white beans

Score the duck skin, rub all over with sea salt and black pepper, then place the fillets skin side down in a cold non-stick frying pan and turn the heat on to medium. Cook for 8 minutes without moving the duck, until the fat is well rendered and the skin is golden and crisp. Turn the duck over and cook for a further 4 minutes, basting with the fat. Meanwhile, pick the sage leaves. Trim the broccoli stalks, halving the stems lengthways. Top and tail the orange, trim off the skin and either slice into rounds or segments, and toss with 1 teaspoon of red wine vinegar and a small pinch of salt and pepper.

When the time's up, remove the duck to a plate to rest, leaving the pan on the heat. Add the sage leaves for 1 minute, or until crispy, jiggling the pan occasionally and transferring them to the duck plate as you go. Cook the broccoli in the pan for 4 minutes, or until lightly charred. Pour in the beans (juices and all), then cover and cook for 3 minutes. Season to perfection, divide between plates and drizzle over any resting juices. Slice the duck and arrange on top, and scatter over the crispy sage and orange.

ENERGY	FAT	SAT FAT	PROTEIN	CARBS	SUGARS	SALT	FIBRE
479kcal	16g	4.1g	54.1g	29.9g	12.1g	1.2g	11.7g

JUICY CHARRED CHICKEN
FLUFFY COUSCOUS, EASY POMEGRANATE, CUCUMBER & MINT SALSA

Celebrating some of the flavours common on the Levantine coast, as well as speed and excitement, just a kiss of pomegranate juice will give you gnarly, caramelized chicken with the juiciest inside.

SERVES 4 | **TOTAL 20 MINUTES**

1 bunch of mint (30g)

300g wholewheat couscous

1 large ripe pomegranate

1 cucumber

4 x 150g skinless chicken breasts

Tear off the top leafy half of the mint, then finely chop and place in a bowl. Put the stalks into another bowl with the couscous, just cover with boiling kettle water, season with sea salt and cover. Leave to hydrate. Halve the pomegranate and, holding one half cut side down in your fingers, bash the back of it with a spoon so all the seeds tumble into the mint bowl, then repeat with the other half. Cut the cucumber into ½cm dice and add to the bowl with 2 tablespoons each of extra virgin olive oil and red wine vinegar. Toss well and season to perfection.

Put a large non-stick frying pan on a medium-high heat. Score the chicken breasts lengthways at 1cm intervals, going about halfway through. Rub with 1 tablespoon of olive oil and a pinch of salt and black pepper, then squeeze over the juice from a few pomegranate seeds (nicked from the salsa). Cook for 8 minutes, or until gnarly and cooked through, turning regularly. Discard the mint stalks from the couscous, fluff up with a fork, mix in half the salsa and divide between plates. Slice the chicken and arrange on top, with the remaining salsa and mint leaves. Finish with extra virgin olive oil, if you like.

ENERGY	FAT	SAT FAT	PROTEIN	CARBS	SUGARS	SALT	FIBRE
528kcal	14.6g	2.5g	45.7g	55.1g	3g	0.8g	6.1g

CHICKEN TRAYBAKE
AUBERGINE, SHAWARMA-SPICED RICE, CRUSHED NUTS & DRIED FRUIT

There's something so satisfying about dishes where the oven does all the work. Inspired by flavours from the Levantine coast, the rice and aubergine absorb big flavour from the chicken and spice.

SERVES 2 | **PREP 5 MINUTES** | **COOK 55 MINUTES**

1 aubergine (250g)

4 x 150g chicken thighs, skin on, bone in

50g luxury fruit and nut mix

1 heaped tablespoon shawarma paste

150g basmati rice

Preheat the oven to 200°C. Trim the aubergine and halve lengthways, use the tip of a knife to score down the length of the skin at 1cm intervals, then halve each piece again. Place in a 20cm x 25cm baking dish with the chicken, and toss with 1 tablespoon each of olive oil and red wine vinegar and a pinch of sea salt and black pepper. Roast for 25 minutes. Meanwhile, finely chop the fruit and nuts.

Boil the kettle. Remove the dish from the oven, then stir in the paste, half the fruit and nuts, and the rice. Stir in 300ml of boiling kettle water, then return to the oven for 25 minutes, or until the rice is cooked and the chicken pulls easily away from the bone. Give the rice a little fork up, sprinkle over the remaining chopped fruit and nuts, and serve.

ENERGY	FAT	SAT FAT	PROTEIN	CARBS	SUGARS	SALT	FIBRE
816kcal	39g	8.1g	37.7g	82.3g	14.0g	1.1g	8.4g

CHICKEN & CHIPS
STICKY ONIONS, JAMMY ROASTED LEMON & FRESH OREGANO

There's something wonderfully humble about the combo of chicken and potatoes, and inspired by my trips to Greece, this expression of something we know and love is guaranteed to please.

SERVES 4 | **TOTAL 1 HOUR 18 MINUTES**

1kg red-skinned potatoes

2 onions

1 bunch of oregano (20g)

2 lemons

4 x 250g chicken legs

Remove the top shelf from the oven, then preheat to 200°C. Scrub the potatoes, chop into erratic 2 to 5cm chunks and place in a large baking dish. Peel and quarter the onions, then break apart into petals and add to the dish. Strip half the oregano leaves into a pestle and mortar and pound to a paste with a pinch of sea salt and black pepper, then muddle in 2 tablespoons each of olive oil and red wine vinegar. Drizzle most of the marinade into the dish, toss together well and roast for 10 minutes.

Meanwhile, use a speed-peeler to strip the peel from the lemons, then slice the lemons in half. Toss the chicken legs in the reserved marinade. When the time's up, arrange the chicken directly on the bars of the top shelf and return it to the oven, so the delicious juices rain down on to the spuds below. Throw the lemon halves into the baking dish, then roast for 1 hour, or until everything is golden, shaking up the potatoes and onions halfway and tossing through the remaining oregano leaves and lemon strips for the last 15 minutes. Carefully remove the chicken from the oven, along with the veg, and squeeze over the jammy roasted lemon halves, to serve.

ENERGY	FAT	SAT FAT	PROTEIN	CARBS	SUGARS	SALT	FIBRE
615kcal	30.2g	7.2g	38g	50.8g	6.8g	0.9g	4.6g

MEAT

RIOJA SHORT RIBS
RICH RED WINE & TOMATO SAUCE, STICKY MARMALADE GLAZE

I love cooking short ribs! You can buy them easily from your butcher, and they'll give you the most melt-in-the-mouth meat, but also the incredible flavour from the bones gives the sauce a real depth.

SERVES 6 | **TOTAL 4 HOURS 35 MINUTES**

6 beef short ribs, bone in (approx. 1.5kg total)

600g frozen chopped mixed onion, carrot and celery

300ml Rioja red wine

3 x 400g tins of plum tomatoes

3 teaspoons coarse-cut dark Seville orange marmalade

Preheat the oven to 160°C. Place a large non-stick frying pan on a medium-high heat. Season the ribs very generously with black pepper and a pinch of sea salt, then toss to coat. Place in the hot pan with 1 tablespoon of olive oil and brown all over for 10 minutes, turning regularly with tongs, then remove to a snug-fitting high-sided roasting tray or casserole pan, bone side down. Tip the frozen mixed veg into the frying pan juices and cook for a further 10 minutes to soften, then pour in the wine and allow most of it to bubble and cook away. Add the tomatoes, breaking them up with a potato masher, then half fill each tin with water, swirl around and pour into the tray. Bring to the boil and season lightly with salt and pepper. Pour the sauce over the ribs, then cover and cook in the oven for 4 hours, or until the meat is beautifully tender, basting occasionally and adding splashes of water, if needed.

When the meat's tender, spoon the excess fat off the tray into a jam jar (save for tasty cooking another day). Heat the marmalade in a pan with a splash of water, then, taking pride, spoon it over the meat and bone of the short ribs, and put back into the oven for 10 minutes to set the glaze. Serve with a carb of your choice and some steamed seasonal greens.

ENERGY	FAT	SAT FAT	PROTEIN	CARBS	SUGARS	SALT	FIBRE
540kcal	35.6g	15.2g	34g	12.2g	11.2g	0.8g	3.4g

HERBY STEAK & CRISPY POTATOES
GREEN PESTO, JUICY MIXED-COLOUR TOMATO SALAD & CRUSHED PISTACHIOS

Inspired by pistou, a beautiful French condiment made with smashed basil, garlic and oil, this tasty dish is a joy to eat. I've swapped in pesto for ease, but buy fresh for amplified flavour and texture.

SERVES 2 | **TOTAL 30 MINUTES**

500g red-skinned potatoes

1 x 300g sirloin steak

4 teaspoons fresh green pesto or pistou

6 ripe medium mixed-colour tomatoes

20g shelled unsalted pistachios

Scrub the potatoes, chop into 2cm chunks, then place in a large non-stick frying pan on a medium heat with 2 tablespoons of olive oil and season with sea salt and black pepper. Fry for 20 minutes, or until golden and cooked through, stirring regularly, then remove to a bowl. Put the pan back on a high heat.

Cut the fat off the steak, then roughly chop the fat and place in the pan to render. Generously season the steak, rub all over with 2 teaspoons of pesto, and cook for 3 minutes on each side for medium rare, or to your liking. Remove to a plate to rest. Return the potatoes to the pan to warm through, while you slice the tomatoes 1cm thick and arrange on serving plates. Dress with a splash of red wine vinegar and a drizzle of extra virgin olive oil, and season to perfection. Spoon over the potatoes, then slice and divide up the steak, pouring over any resting juices. Spoon over the remaining pesto, then bash and scatter over the pistachios. Finish with a drizzle of extra virgin olive oil, if you like.

ENERGY	FAT	SAT FAT	PROTEIN	CARBS	SUGARS	SALT	FIBRE
735kcal	42.1g	11.7g	40g	51.8g	9.5g	1.4g	6.4g

CREAMY MUSTARDY PORK
GOLDEN MIXED MUSHROOMS, CRÈME FRAÎCHE & PEPPERY ROCKET

This is one of those really fast, impressive meals inspired by my time spent cooking and eating in France. People always think sauces are complicated, but this one comes together in no time at all.

SERVES 2 | **TOTAL 10 MINUTES**

300g pork fillet

200g mixed mushrooms

1 heaped tablespoon wholegrain mustard

2 heaped tablespoons crème fraîche

40g rocket

Place a large non-stick frying pan on a high heat. Slice the pork into 6 medallions, bashing to flatten slightly, and roughly slice the mushrooms. Place them in the pan with 1 tablespoon of olive oil and cook for 2 minutes on each side, or until the mushrooms are golden and the pork is just cooked through, then remove just the mushrooms to a plate. Go in with the mustard and crème fraîche and cook for 1 last minute, loosening with a splash of water, if needed. Taste and season to perfection with sea salt and black pepper, divide between plates, then scatter over the golden mushrooms and rocket, and finish with a drizzle of extra virgin olive oil. Nice served with rice.

ENERGY	FAT	SAT FAT	PROTEIN	CARBS	SUGARS	SALT	FIBRE
370kcal	23.9g	8.9g	36.8g	1.9g	1.5g	1.2g	1.4g

ROLLED BRAISED STEAKS
TAPENADE & TALEGGIO STUFFING, RICH TOMATO SAUCE

There's something really special about elevating a cheaper cut of meat, like topside of beef, by rolling it up with thoughtful flavour combos, then slow-cooking until scrumptious and tender. I just love it.

SERVES 6 | TOTAL 1 HOUR 30 MINUTES

6 x 150g topside minute steaks (ask your butcher)

6 teaspoons black olive tapenade

100g Taleggio cheese

1 sprig of sage

2 x 400g jars of tomato and red wine sauce

Preheat the oven to 180°C. Place one of the steaks between two pieces of greaseproof paper, then use a rolling pin to evenly bash it out to just under ½cm thick. Repeat with the rest of the steaks, then lay them all out on a clean work surface. Spread 1 teaspoon of tapenade over the surface of each steak, tear over the Taleggio, then roll up and secure with a piece of butcher's string.

Pick the sage leaves into a large casserole pan on a medium-high heat with 3 tablespoons of olive oil and fry until crispy, then remove to kitchen paper. Add the rolled steaks to the pan and brown all over for 4 minutes, then pour in the two jars of sauce. Half fill each jar with water, swirl around and tip into the pan. Bring to a simmer, then cover and place in the oven for 1 hour. Remove the lid, turn the steaks over, then cook for a further 20 minutes without the lid, or until the steaks are tender when pinched. Remove the steaks to a board, then snip off and discard the strings. Skim any fat from the surface of the sauce and drizzle it over the steaks. Taste and season the sauce to perfection, pour on to a large serving platter, then slice up the steaks and arrange them across the top. Scatter with the crispy sage leaves and serve. Amazing as is, or with bread, mash, polenta or spaghetti.

ENERGY	FAT	SAT FAT	PROTEIN	CARBS	SUGARS	SALT	FIBRE
515kcal	35.6g	12.6g	35.8g	11.8g	7.2g	2.1g	2g

STUFFED ONIONS
HERBY SAUSAGE & FETA FILLING, TOMATO RICE

Across the Greek islands they stuff many different vegetables with grains, herbs and all kinds of wonderful things, and this is my version, celebrating the best of onions filled with simple ingredients.

SERVES 4 | **TOTAL 1 HOUR 10 MINUTES**

4 large mixed onions

6 herby sausages (400g total)

60g feta cheese

1 x 400g tin of plum tomatoes

250g basmati rice

Preheat the oven to 200°C. Peel the onions and halve widthways across the middle, then place in a large shallow casserole pan. Season with sea salt and black pepper, drizzle over 1 tablespoon of olive oil, then roast for 30 minutes. Squeeze the sausagemeat into a bowl, discarding the skins, scrunch in most of the feta, then put aside. When the time's up on the onions, use tongs to transfer them to a board. Carefully remove and roughly chop the cores, then add just the chopped onion to the pan and place over a medium heat. Scrunch in the tomatoes through clean hands and pour in 1 tin's worth of water, bring to a simmer, then add the rice, and mix together well.

Unclick and separate the onions into rings (like you can see in the picture), then roughly divide the sausage mixture between the rings. Arrange nicely on top of the rice, squashing them in, right up to the edges to cover the rice. Drizzle with 1 tablespoon of olive oil, then roast for 20 minutes, or until golden on top and the rice is cooked through. Crumble over the remaining feta and serve up.

ENERGY	FAT	SAT FAT	PROTEIN	CARBS	SUGARS	SALT	FIBRE
630kcal	26.6g	8.5g	24.1g	77.8g	14.6g	2.3g	5.3g

PORK & PEPPERS
CRISPY ARTICHOKES, CHICKPEAS & ARTICHOKE ALIOLI

This is a celebration of Spanish flavours coming together in a beautiful way. Mastering a super-juicy pork chop is key, and my advice is to cook two thick chops for four, instead of four thin dry ones.

SERVES 4 | TOTAL 40 MINUTES

4 mixed-colour peppers (make sure you have 1 red pepper)

1 x 280g jar of artichoke hearts in oil

3 cloves of garlic

2 x 400g thick pork chops, bone in, skin removed and reserved (ask your butcher)

1 x 700g jar of chickpeas

Carefully blacken the peppers over a direct flame on the hob (or on a barbecue or under the grill), turning with tongs until charred all over. Drain the artichokes, reserving the oil. Peel and bash the garlic in a pestle and mortar with a big pinch of sea salt, add 1 teaspoon of red wine vinegar and muddle together. Whisking continuously, slowly add the reserved artichoke oil until thickened and emulsified. Taste and season to perfection with salt and black pepper.

Using a sharp knife, score the fat of the pork chops at ½cm intervals, then season all over with sea salt. Put the two chops together and balance fat side down in a large non-stick frying pan on a medium heat for around 10 minutes, to get the fat crispy and rendering. Turn the chops on to their sides and cook for 5 minutes on each side, or until golden and cooked through, stirring in the artichokes for the last 2 minutes, then remove to a plate. Give the pan a quick wipe and cook the pork skin until crispy. Meanwhile, peel, deseed and slice the peppers, then season with a splash of red wine vinegar and a pinch of salt and pepper. Whiz 1 red pepper in a blender and pour into the pan with the chickpeas (juices and all). Warm through for a couple of minutes, then pour on to a serving platter. Place the pork chops on top, drizzling over any resting juices. Scatter over the peppers and artichokes, and break over the crispy pork skin. Serve the alioli on the side, for drizzling over.

ENERGY	FAT	SAT FAT	PROTEIN	CARBS	SUGARS	SALT	FIBRE
517kcal	31.4g	10.4g	31.8g	26.2g	7.4g	2g	10.7g

TENDER LAMB SHANKS
SMOKY AUBERGINES, SPICED TOMATO & MIXED BEAN STEW

Slow-cooking to achieve melt-in-the-mouth meat is one of my favourite things to do, and this tender lamb dish centred around the North African spice mix ras el hanout is just so incredibly comforting.

SERVES 4 | **PREP 5 MINUTES** | **COOK 3 HOURS 10 MINUTES**

4 lamb shanks (roughly 400g each)

2 tablespoons ras el hanout, plus extra to serve

2 aubergines (250g each)

2 x 400g tins of plum tomatoes

2 x 400g tins of mixed beans

Preheat the oven to 200°C. Rub the lamb shanks all over with 1 tablespoon each of olive oil and red wine vinegar and half the ras el hanout. Place in a large casserole pan and roast for 40 minutes, turning halfway. Meanwhile, prick the aubergines, then carefully blacken them over a direct flame on the hob (or under the grill), turning with tongs until soft inside.

Once cool enough to handle, carefully remove the aubergine skin, adding the flesh to the pan when the roasting time is up. Scrunch in the tomatoes through clean hands, add a pinch of sea salt and black pepper, the remaining ras el hanout and the beans (juices and all), then stir well. Turn the oven down to 160°C, cover and cook for 2 hours 30 minutes, or until meltingly tender and falling off the bone. Dust with extra ras el hanout and serve. Nice as it is, or with rice or warm flatbreads.

ENERGY	FAT	SAT FAT	PROTEIN	CARBS	SUGARS	SALT	FIBRE
704kcal	35g	15.8g	61.4g	33.2g	11.8g	1.7g	14.8g

LAMB MEATBALLS
TZATZIKI & MINT SAUCE, CHARRED RED PEPPERS & LEMON

Walking around the buzzing city of Thessaloniki I saw many different expressions of meatballs in all kinds of shapes and sizes, which inspired this simply beautiful plate – a delicious mezze dish or starter.

SERVES 4 | TOTAL 25 MINUTES

1 lemon

1 x 200g tub of tzatziki

1 bunch of mint (30g)

½ x 460g jar of roasted red peppers

400g minced lamb

Finely grate the lemon zest and put aside. Squeeze half the lemon juice into a blender, add the tzatziki and pick in most of the mint leaves, then whiz to a smooth sauce. Season to perfection with sea salt and black pepper, then put aside. Drain and finely chop one of the peppers, then place in a bowl with half the lemon zest, the lamb, a pinch of salt and plenty of pepper. Scrunch and mix together really well, then divide into 8 and squeeze into long oval-shaped rustic meatballs.

Drizzle 1 tablespoon of olive oil into a large non-stick frying pan on a high heat, then dot in the meatballs and cook for 10 minutes, or until golden and cooked through, turning occasionally. Drain and slice the remaining peppers and add to the pan, in and around the meatballs, for the last 2 minutes, turning halfway. Divide the sauce between plates, top with the meatballs and peppers, then scatter over the remaining lemon zest and mint leaves. Slice the remaining lemon half into wedges, for squeezing over. Delicious served with a hunk of bread for mopping up the sauce.

ENERGY	FAT	SAT FAT	PROTEIN	CARBS	SUGARS	SALT	FIBRE
241kcal	15.5g	6.4g	21.7g	3.6g	2.8g	0.6g	0.7g

SUMPTUOUS PORK STEW
CRISPY SAGE, ONION, SWEET TOMATOES & SQUASH MASH

This stew is simplicity itself. The flavour I'm trying to create is what the Italians call *agrodolce* – sweet and sour: sweetness from the slow-cooked onions, and sourness from cooking away the vinegar.

SERVES 4 | **TOTAL 3 HOURS**

2 sprigs of sage

600g pork cheeks or shoulder steaks

3 onions

2 x 400g tins of plum tomatoes

1 large butternut squash (1.5kg)

Preheat the oven to 160°C. Pick the sage leaves into a large casserole pan on a medium heat with 3 tablespoons of olive oil and fry until crispy, then remove to kitchen paper, leaving the flavoured oil behind. Slice the pork into 2cm chunks, toss with 2 teaspoons of black pepper and a pinch of sea salt, then brown in the pan while you peel, roughly chop and add the onions. Add a good swig of red wine vinegar, then cook for 20 minutes, or until dark and caramelized, stirring occasionally. Scrunch in the tomatoes through clean hands, then pour in 2 tins' worth of water. Pop the lid on, cook in the oven for 2 hours 30 minutes, or until beautifully tender, then taste and season to perfection.

With 1 hour 15 minutes to go, halve and deseed the squash, transfer it to a baking tray, then rub all over with 1 tablespoon of olive oil and a pinch of salt and pepper. Place in the oven to roast until tender, and add a splash of water to the stew, if needed. To serve, scoop out the soft squash flesh and plate up alongside the stew, scattered with the crispy sage leaves.

ENERGY	FAT	SAT FAT	PROTEIN	CARBS	SUGARS	SALT	FIBRE
636kcal	35g	9.4g	34.8g	49.2g	32.0g	0.9g	10.2g

GIANT BAKED BEANS
MINI SAUSAGE MEATBALLS, SWEET TOMATOES & TANGY FETA

Mediterraneans love their beans – all kinds of different varieties – and inspired by some delicious mezze I had in Thessaloniki, I came up with this very simple, tasty dish that we all love at home.

SERVES 6 | **TOTAL 50 MINUTES**

6 spicy pork sausages or veggie alternative (400g total)

320g frozen chopped mixed onion, carrot and celery

1 x 700g jar of giant butter beans or 2 x 400g tins of butter beans

2 x 400g tins of plum tomatoes

200g feta cheese

Preheat the oven to 180°C. Place a large non-stick ovenproof frying pan on a medium heat with 1 tablespoon of olive oil. Pull the sausagemeat out of the skins into rustic 3cm balls and put straight into the pan. Brown all over for 3 minutes, then remove to a plate. Place the frozen mixed veg in the pan and cook for 10 minutes, stirring regularly, then tip in the beans (juices and all). Scrunch in the tomatoes through clean hands, season with black pepper, then bring to the boil. Finely break up and stir through half the feta, dot in the sausage meatballs, then coarsely break the rest of the feta into chunks and scatter on top. Bake for 25 minutes, or until golden, thick and blipping away. I love it served as is, or with a hunk of fresh bread for dunking and mopping up the sauce.

ENERGY	FAT	SAT FAT	PROTEIN	CARBS	SUGARS	SALT	FIBRE
571kcal	34.6g	13.3g	31.4g	32.9g	12.6g	2g	10.6g

STEAK TAGLIATA
GLAZED BALSAMIC BEETROOTS, GOAT'S CHEESE & TARRAGON

Here, I'm celebrating a cheaper cut of steak — cooked medium-rare, sliced thinly, then buddied with the undeniable flavours of sweet beets and balsamic, and goat's cheese and tarragon, it's a real treat.

SERVES 2 | TOTAL 16 MINUTES

180g vac-packed cooked beetroot (no vinegar)

1 x 300g skirt steak, such as onglet

4 tablespoons thick balsamic vinegar

70g soft goat's cheese

½ a bunch of tarragon (10g)

Trim, then slice the beets ½cm thick. Preheat a large non-stick frying pan on a high heat. Season the steak with sea salt and black pepper, place in the pan with 1 tablespoon of olive oil and fry for 5 minutes, or until medium-rare, turning and moving it around the pan regularly, then remove to a plate to rest. Put the beets into the pan, then drizzle in the balsamic and toss for a few minutes, to glaze. Divide the beets between serving plates, then thinly slice and layer over the goat's cheese. Slice the steak thinly across the grain and divide between the plates, drizzling over any resting juices. Pick the tarragon leaves, toss in a little extra virgin olive oil and red wine vinegar, then scatter over the top.

ENERGY	FAT	SAT FAT	PROTEIN	CARBS	SUGARS	SALT	FIBRE
523kcal	30g	13g	42.9g	19.4g	18.4g	1.4g	1.7g

PULLED LAMB SHOULDER
BAHARAT SPICES, PICKLED VEG, FLATBREADS & HOUMOUS

A wonderful feasting dish, celebrating Eastern Mediterranean baharat spices, with quick-pickled veg, homemade flatbreads, houmous dressing and meltingly tender meat – it really is a spectacular meal.

SERVES 10 | PREP 5 MINUTES | COOK 5 HOURS

1 x 42g jar of baharat spice mix

1 x 3kg lamb shoulder, bone in

1kg self-raising flour

2 x 320g packs of pepper, onion, carrot and cabbage stir-fry mix

2 x 200g tubs of houmous

Preheat the oven to 150°C. Mix most of the spice mix with 2 tablespoons each of olive oil and red wine vinegar and a good pinch of sea salt and black pepper, then rub all over the lamb. Place in a roasting tray with a good splash of water, cover tightly with tin foil, then roast for 5 hours, or until beautifully tender and pullable. Remove the foil, baste with the juices, then roast for a final 20 minutes.

Meanwhile, put the flour into a bowl with a small pinch of sea salt, then gradually add 600ml of water, mixing with a fork as you go. Tip on to a flour-dusted surface and knead for a few minutes, until smooth. Divide the dough into 10, then place on a flour-dusted tray and cover with a damp cloth, until needed. Tip the veg mix into a large bowl and dress with 4 tablespoons of red wine vinegar and a good pinch of salt and pepper. Toss and leave aside to pickle. With 30 minutes to go, roll the dough into rounds, roughly 25cm in diameter. Dry-fry in a large non-stick frying pan on a high heat until golden and puffed up – you'll need to work in batches. Keep warm under a clean tea towel. Drain off the lamb fat (keep in a jam jar for tasty cooking another day). Stir a good splash of boiling kettle water into the meat juices, scraping any sticky bits from the bottom of the tray. Transfer the houmous to a serving bowl with a pinch of spice and let it down with a good splash of water, then shred the lamb, discarding the bones, and toss in the tray juices. To serve, load the flatbreads with pickled veg, shredded lamb, houmous dressing and a pinch of spice.

ENERGY	FAT	SAT FAT	PROTEIN	CARBS	SUGARS	SALT	FIBRE
923kcal	46.1g	17.7g	44.2g	84.6g	5.4g	2.2g	8.6g

PORK & PRUNES
SWEET CARROTS & CRISPY ROSEMARY CRACKLING

The beautiful Greek island of Skopelos hails dried prunes as one of its most prized ingredients and they use them in so many tasty ways, like in this rustic stew, to bring deep sweet-savouriness.

SERVES 6 | TOTAL 2 HOURS 15 MINUTES

1.5kg pork belly, skin and ribs removed and reserved (ask your butcher)

½ a bunch of rosemary (10g)

1 heaped tablespoon ground coriander

800g mixed-colour carrots

200g prunes (stoned)

Preheat the oven to 220°C. To make the crackling, roll up the pork skin and use a sharp knife to cut it into 1cm slices, then place in a deep roasting tray. Toss with a good pinch of sea salt and black pepper, then roast for 20 minutes, or until golden and crisp, stripping in and stirring through half the rosemary leaves for the last 5 minutes. Remove to kitchen paper and put aside, then reduce the oven to 160°C.

Meanwhile, slice the rest of the pork belly into 2.5cm chunks, then toss the belly and ribs with a pinch of salt, 1 teaspoon of pepper and the ground coriander. Fry in a large casserole pan on a high heat with 1 tablespoon of olive oil until golden all over, turning regularly, while you slice the carrots into 3cm chunks and roughly chop the prunes. Add to the pan, then pick and finely chop the remaining rosemary. Keep everything moving for 5 minutes to accentuate the colour, add a splash of red wine vinegar, then pour in 600ml of boiling water and stir well. Cover and cook gently in the oven for 1 hour 30 minutes, or until beautifully tender, stirring halfway and adding a splash of water, if needed. Serve the stew with the crispy crackling on top. Delicious with bread, rice or potatoes.

ENERGY	FAT	SAT FAT	PROTEIN	CARBS	SUGARS	SALT	FIBRE
671kcal	44.8g	15.6g	42.2g	26.8g	19.2g	1.3g	5.8g

PORK ESCALOPE
FRIED EGG, MARINATED OLIVES & LEMON

Delicately breaded meat fried until crisp and juicy is enjoyed all over the Mediterranean. Served with a much-loved soft-cooked egg, salty olives and a hit of zingy lemon juice, this is truly scrumptious.

SERVES 2 | **TOTAL 20 MINUTES**

100g fine dried breadcrumbs

3 large eggs

1 x 300g pork fillet

8 mixed marinated olives

½ a lemon

Tip the breadcrumbs on to a large plate, and whisk 1 egg in a shallow bowl. Slice the fillet into 4 equal pieces. One at a time, use your fist or a rolling pin to bash out and tenderize each piece of pork between sheets of greaseproof paper, to ½cm thick. Season with sea salt and black pepper, dip each piece in the egg, letting any excess drip off, then turn in the breadcrumbs, pressing to coat. Chop the olives (destone, if needed), plus any of the marinating ingredients, and slice the lemon into wedges.

I like to cook a portion at a time: place 2 escalopes in a large non-stick pan on a medium-high heat with a good splash of olive oil and cook for 1½ minutes on each side, or until golden and cooked through, frying 1 egg alongside after the second flip, to your liking – angle the pan and spoon any excess oil over the egg to help it cook. Remove the escalopes to a plate lined with kitchen paper to drain, then plate up, and top with the fried egg. Scatter over half the olives, then repeat with the remaining ingredients. Serve with lemon wedges for squeezing over.

ENERGY	FAT	SAT FAT	PROTEIN	CARBS	SUGARS	SALT	FIBRE
492kcal	16.8g	5g	60.7g	24.4g	2.1g	1.8g	1.1g

LAMB TANGIA
SPICED TOMATO & OLIVE BROTH & VERMICELLI RICE NOODLES

This has to be one of the easiest, most delicious dishes that you can put together and just let blip away in the oven, developing rich, beautiful flavour over time that the noodles can go on to absorb.

SERVES 4 | **PREP 15 MINUTES** | **COOK 3 HOURS**

1.2kg lamb neck, bone in, sliced

2 tablespoons ras el hanout, plus extra to serve

1kg ripe mixed-colour tomatoes

100g mixed marinated olives

3 nests of vermicelli (150g)

Preheat the oven to 180°C. Place the lamb neck in a large pot (or tangia) with the ras el hanout. Quarter and deseed the tomatoes, adding the tomato petals to the pot, along with the olives (and marinating ingredients). Pour over 1.5 litres of boiling kettle water, pop the lid on and cook in the oven for 3 hours, or until the lamb is tender and falling off the bone. Taste and season the broth to perfection, crumble in the noodles, making sure they're submerged, then cover and wait 5 minutes for the noodles to rehydrate and absorb the tasty broth. To serve, remove and shred the lamb, discarding any gristly bits and bones, and return the lamb to the pot. Toss together, and finish with a drizzle of extra virgin olive oil and an extra dusting of ras el hanout.

ENERGY	FAT	SAT FAT	PROTEIN	CARBS	SUGARS	SALT	FIBRE
544kcal	24.2g	10.2g	34.2g	46.8g	8g	1.8g	3.4g

BALSAMIC PORK STEW

CELERY, MIXED SPICE, BLACK PEPPER, ONION & TOMATO SAUCE

This comforting Italian stew has a real depth of flavour and layers of gentle spice. Plus, slow-cooking pork and vinegar is a total joy. Any leftovers can be gratefully tossed through pasta and Parmesan.

SERVES 8 TO 10 | **PREP 5 MINUTES** | **COOK 3 HOURS 15 MINUTES**

2kg pork shoulder steaks

1 head of celery

2 x 454g jars of pickled onions in balsamic vinegar

3 heaped teaspoons mixed spice

2 x 400g tins of plum tomatoes

Preheat the oven to 150°C. Cut the pork steaks in half and toss with a good pinch of sea salt and 1 tablespoon of black pepper. Place in a large casserole pan on a high heat with 2 tablespoons of olive oil and cook until golden brown, stirring regularly, then remove to a plate – you'll need to work in batches. Meanwhile, trim, peel and roughly chop the celery, reserving the inner yellow leaves in cold water. Drain and halve the onions, reserving the balsamic vinegar from the jar.

Add the celery, mixed spice and onions to the pan juices with 5 tablespoons of the balsamic vinegar (don't throw the rest away, it's fantastic for making salad dressings). Cook the vinegar away, then put the pork back into the pan with the tomatoes, breaking them up with a spoon. Pour in 2 tins' worth of water, bring to a simmer, then cover and cook in the oven for 2 hours. Remove the lid, give everything a quick stir and cook for a further 1 hour, or until beautifully tender. Season to perfection, then drain and scatter over the celery leaves. Delicious served with bread, orzo, mash, polenta or rice.

ENERGY	FAT	SAT FAT	PROTEIN	CARBS	SUGARS	SALT	FIBRE
484kcal	29.6g	9.8g	48.6g	6.8g	6g	1.7g	1.8g

SWEET THINGS

JOOLS' CHOCOLATE DREAMS
SILKY-SMOOTH CHOCOLATE, BEST COFFEE, PURE HAPPINESS

Chocolate and coffee are celebrated all around the Med and they're also my wife's two favourite indulgent pleasures, so why wouldn't I create possibly one of the most decadent desserts on earth?

SERVES 6 | **TOTAL 40 MINUTES, PLUS COOLING**

150g dark chocolate (70%)

125g unsalted butter

50ml good espresso

2 large eggs

125g golden caster sugar

Preheat the oven to 120°C. Snap the chocolate into a heatproof bowl, add the butter, espresso and a good pinch of sea salt, and place over a pan of gently simmering water to melt very slowly until smooth, stirring regularly. Meanwhile, whisk the eggs and sugar together until pale and doubled in size, then carefully fold in the melted chocolate mixture.

Boil the kettle. Divide the mixture between 6 coffee cups or ramekins and put them into a roasting tray. Place the tray in the oven, then carefully pour in enough boiling kettle water to come halfway up the side of the cups. Bake for exactly 20 minutes, then carefully remove from the oven and leave to cool in the water for 2 hours. To serve, I sometimes shave over some extra chocolate, or add fresh fruit like cherries, blood oranges or wild strawberries, with a dollop of yoghurt or crème fraîche.

ENERGY	FAT	SAT FAT	PROTEIN	CARBS	SUGARS	SALT	FIBRE
400kcal	26.8g	15.9g	3.8g	38.6g	38.5g	0.4g	0.0g

EASY FIG TART
FRUIT & NUT BASE, VANILLA YOGHURT & HONEY

Take the fuss out of creating a show-stopping dessert with this super-quick no-cook fig tart – a delicate base of crushed fruit and nuts, topped with yoghurt, figs and a drizzle of honey.

SERVES 8 | **TOTAL 10 MINUTES, PLUS FREEZING**

300g luxury fruit and nut mix

500g Greek yoghurt

1 teaspoon vanilla bean paste

1 teaspoon runny honey, plus extra to serve

4 perfectly ripe figs

Line a 20cm springform cake tin with greaseproof paper. Tip the fruit and nuts into a food processor and blitz until fine and tacky (it should be easy to mould with your hands), then push and press it into the base of the lined tin, and 2.5cm up the sides. Leave to firm up in the freezer for 1 hour. When the time's up, mix the yoghurt with the vanilla and 1 teaspoon of honey, then spoon into the chilled tart case. Freeze for 1 further hour, or until slightly set. Release the tart from the tin, halve or quarter the figs and arrange nicely on top, then drizzle generously with honey, to finish.

ENERGY	FAT	SAT FAT	PROTEIN	CARBS	SUGARS	SALT	FIBRE
272kcal	16.3g	4.7g	7.2g	23.3g	22.6g	0.1g	2.5g

APPLE TART
STICKY APRICOT GLAZE, FLAKED ALMONDS & ICE CREAM

Inspired by the classic French tartelettes you can find in pâtisseries, I'm using shop-bought pastry for convenience. Topped with vanilla ice cream, this is a lovely little number to have up your sleeve.

SERVES 8 | **TOTAL 50 MINUTES**

320g sheet of ready-rolled puff pastry (cold)

200g apricot jam

4 eating apples

1 tablespoon flaked almonds

vanilla ice cream, to serve

Preheat the oven to 200°C. Unroll the pastry sheet on its paper and place on a baking tray, then score a 1cm border around the edge (don't cut all the way through). Heat the jam in a pan over a low heat for 30 seconds, just to loosen, stirring occasionally. Very finely slice the apples into rounds, discarding any pips (use a mandolin, with a guard, if you have one). Toss the apple with the apricot jam and arrange nicely, in layers, inside the border, hiding any smaller tattier bits of apple underneath. Cook at the bottom of the oven for 30 minutes, or until beautifully golden and cooked through, scattering over the almonds for the last 5 minutes. Slice up and serve topped with balls of vanilla ice cream.

ENERGY	FAT	SAT FAT	PROTEIN	CARBS	SUGARS	SALT	FIBRE
262kcal	11.1g	5g	3.1g	45g	21.1g	0.4g	1.7g

CRÈME CARAMEL
SWEET VANILLA CUSTARD & PASSION FRUIT

Sometimes nothing beats an old-school classic like the crème caramel. Serving up this popular dessert with magical passion fruit gives it a fresh and fruity twist to really cut through the indulgence.

SERVES 6 | **TOTAL 1 HOUR, PLUS CHILLING**

160g caster sugar

1 vanilla pod

600ml whole milk

6 large eggs

3 ripe passion fruit

Preheat the oven to 150°C and line a deep roasting tray with greaseproof paper, then place 6 ramekins or ovenproof moulds inside. Sprinkle 100g of the sugar into a non-stick frying pan, add 3 tablespoons of water and place on a medium heat for about 8 minutes, or until you've got a chestnut brown caramel – don't be tempted to stir or taste it, just gently swirl the pan occasionally. Quickly and carefully divide the caramel between the ramekins. Halve the vanilla pod lengthways and scrape out the seeds, then put both the pod and seeds into a saucepan, along with the milk. Bring almost to the boil, then switch off the heat. Meanwhile, place 2 whole eggs and 4 egg yolks in a bowl (save the whites for making meringues another day) and whisk with the remaining sugar for 1 minute. Slowly pour in the hot milk, whisking continuously. Discard the vanilla pod, and skim away any foam from the top.

Divide the custard between the ramekins, then carefully half-fill the tray with boiling kettle water and bake for 30 minutes, or until just set and a sharp knife comes out clean. Leave to cool completely in the water, then remove, cover and transfer the crème caramels to the fridge for at least 4 hours, or overnight. To serve, dip the base of each ramekin into a bowl of boiling water for 1 minute to loosen, then run a knife around the edge and confidently turn out on to a plate, shaking slightly to loosen, if needed. Squeeze half a passion fruit over each, to serve.

ENERGY	FAT	SAT FAT	PROTEIN	CARBS	SUGARS	SALT	FIBRE
256kcal	10.1g	4.2g	10.6g	32.9g	32.9g	0.3g	0g

LEMON CURD TART
CITRUS-SWIRLED PASTRY & FRESH RASPBERRIES

Many wonderful desserts in the Med celebrate the bounty of citrus. I've embellished this lemon tart by rolling and flavouring pastry to create amazing texture, as the Portuguese and French do so well.

SERVES 6 | **TOTAL 30 MINUTES**

120g icing sugar, plus extra for dusting

320g sheet of ready-rolled puff pastry (cold)

5 lemons (120ml juice total)

4 large eggs

150g raspberries

Preheat the oven to 190°C. Dust a clean work surface with icing sugar, then unroll the puff pastry, discarding the paper. Dust the pastry with icing sugar and finely grate over the zest of 2 lemons, then roll it tightly back up and slice into 1cm discs. Rub a 24cm non-stick ovenproof frying pan with olive oil, then distribute the pastry discs around the sides and base, pressing them together really well to create one piece of pastry. Bake on the bottom of the oven for 20 minutes, or until lightly golden.

Meanwhile, finely grate the zest from the remaining lemons into a large heatproof bowl, and squeeze in all the juice (you'll need 120ml). Whisk in the icing sugar and eggs, then place the bowl over a pan of simmering water on a medium heat. Whisk continuously for around 10 minutes, or until thickened, then remove from the heat. Pour the lemon curd into the pastry case, then finish under a hot grill for a few minutes (cover any pastry edges with tin foil, if it starts getting too dark). Serve at room temperature, with a few fresh raspberries scattered on top and the rest on the side.

ENERGY	FAT	SAT FAT	PROTEIN	CARBS	SUGARS	SALT	FIBRE
341kcal	16.8g	7.5g	8.1g	51.3g	22.7g	0.6g	1.6g

TAHINI ROCKY ROAD
JAM RIPPLE, CRUSHED BISCUITS, FRUIT & NUTS

One of the joys of travelling is that you come across amazing ingredient combos, and most of the fun is in incorporating them into your own family classics – this beauty happened after my trip to Tunisia.

SERVES 12 | **TOTAL 20 MINUTES, PLUS CHILLING**

300g dark chocolate (70%)

4 tablespoons tahini

300g luxury fruit and nut mix

200g shortbread biscuits

2 tablespoons fruit jam

Sit a heatproof bowl on top of a pan of lightly simmering water, snap in the chocolate, add 3 tablespoons of tahini, and stir occasionally until melted. Meanwhile, roughly chop just half the fruit and nuts and all the biscuits, then combine with the remaining fruit and nuts. Fold most of the mix into the melted chocolate, reserving a small handful for decoration later. Pour into a baking dish lined with greaseproof paper (one that'll hold the mixture at around 2.5cm thick) and sprinkle over the handful of reserved fruit, nuts and biscuits. Add blobs of jam and the remaining tahini and swirl them through. Place in the fridge to cool, harden and set for a few hours, then slice up and serve.

ENERGY	FAT	SAT FAT	PROTEIN	CARBS	SUGARS	SALT	FIBRE
381kcal	23.5g	8.6g	6.3g	36.7g	27.8g	0.2g	2.5g

PISTACHIO PANNA COTTA
SWEET ORANGE & HONEY SYRUP, ORANGE SEGMENTS & BASHED PISTACHIOS

Panna cotta is one of the most famous Italian desserts, and on the island of Sicily you get some wonderful Arabic influences coming through, which I think you subtly taste in the flavours here.

SERVES 8 | **TOTAL 30 MINUTES, PLUS CHILLING**

3 leaves of gelatine

700ml whole milk

200g shelled unsalted pistachios

4 large juicy oranges

4 tablespoons runny honey

Soak the gelatine leaves in cold water until softened. Pour the milk into a pan and add most of the pistachios. Speed-peel in the zest from 1 orange, then add 2 tablespoons of honey and mix well. Bring just to the boil, then remove from the heat and leave to cool for 10 minutes. Pick out the orange zest and pour the milk mixture into a blender. Squeeze the water out of the gelatine, add to the blender and leave to dissolve, then blitz for 3 minutes, or until silky-smooth. Pour into 8 serving moulds or small glasses. Cover and chill for at least 5 hours, or until set.

Meanwhile, squeeze the juice of 2 oranges into a small pan, then segment the remaining 2. Drizzle 2 tablespoons of honey into the pan, then reduce over a medium heat until you have a light syrup – about 7 minutes. Bash the remaining pistachios. When you're ready to serve, turn each panna cotta out on to a little plate or saucer – the easiest way to do this is to carefully dip each mould into a bowl of boiling water for around 10 seconds, or until you get a wiggle, then place a plate on top and confidently flip out. Serve with the orange segments, syrup and pistachios.

ENERGY	FAT	SAT FAT	PROTEIN	CARBS	SUGARS	SALT	FIBRE
255kcal	16.7g	3.8g	10.6g	16.5g	16g	0.1g	1.6g

KINDA BAKLAVA

CRISPY FILO, RICE NOODLES, NUTS, FRUIT, ORANGE & HONEY

I've had the privilege of trying all kinds of baklava, flavoured in many beautiful ways, and this is my 5-ingredient homage, using accessible ingredients and a simple method for max flavour and texture.

SERVES 10 TO 12 | **TOTAL 45 MINUTES, PLUS COOLING**

3 large juicy oranges

1 x 340g jar of runny honey

2 nests of vermicelli (100g)

300g luxury fruit and nut mix

1 x 270g pack of filo pastry

Finely grate half the orange zest into a large non-stick frying pan and squeeze in all the juice. Add the honey and place on a medium heat until syrupy, gently swirling the pan occasionally (careful – it's hot!). Leave aside to cool. Preheat the oven to 170°C. Cover the vermicelli with boiling kettle water to soften, then drain, squeezing out any excess liquid. Meanwhile, tip half the fruit and nuts into a food processor and blitz until super-fine, then add the rest and pulse a few times – you want a mixture of fine and chunky. Put a small handful of the mixture aside for later, then tip the vermicelli into the food processor and pulse a few times. Rub a 30cm non-stick ovenproof frying pan with olive oil, lightly rub half the filo sheets with oil, then layer into the pan, leaving the pastry overhanging. Evenly scatter over the vermicelli and nut mixture, then lightly rub the remaining filo with oil, layer them over and tuck in the edges, pressing to compact – there's no need to be neat. Carefully pre-slice into portions, any way you like, then bake for 30 minutes, scattering over the remaining fruit and nuts for the last 5 minutes.

Remove from the oven, use a fish slice to gently press down on the pastry, then evenly pour over the syrup and leave to cool for 2 hours. When you're ready to serve, place on a very low heat to release the baklava, then either serve from the pan or carefully and confidently turn out on to a board.

ENERGY	FAT	SAT FAT	PROTEIN	CARBS	SUGARS	SALT	FIBRE
332kcal	9.2g	1.5g	6.7g	58.5g	30.8g	0.2g	1.9g

LEMON SHERBET
AMARETTI CRUMB, SQUASHED BLACKBERRIES

In the baking hot Mediterranean sun there's probably nothing more refreshing than an iced dessert, and this is an interesting recipe where the citrus gives the dairy a wonderful sherbety fizz. Delicious!

SERVES 6 | **TOTAL 10 MINUTES, PLUS FREEZING**

5 lemons (200ml juice total)

1 x 397g tin of condensed milk

2 tablespoons crème fraîche

150g blackberries

70g Amaretti biscuits

Finely grate the lemon zest on to a tray and leave to dry, for garnish. Squeeze all the juice into a bowl (you'll need 200ml), discarding any pips. Mix in most of the condensed milk, the crème fraîche and 250ml of water, then scrape into a freezer container or a large loaf tin and cover. Freeze for 4 hours, then blitz in a food processor and freeze again until you have a scoopable consistency.

When you're ready to serve, whiz the blackberries until super-smooth with the remaining condensed milk, loosening with a splash of water, if needed. Crush the Amaretti biscuits to a very fine crumb, spoon nicely on to serving plates, then scoop the lemon sherbet on top. Sprinkle over the reserved lemon zest and serve the blackberry sauce alongside.

ENERGY	FAT	SAT FAT	PROTEIN	CARBS	SUGARS	SALT	FIBRE
284kcal	9.8g	4.9g	7g	44.3g	44.1g	0.2g	1.5g

SIMPLE CELEBRATION CAKE
PANETTONE, RICOTTA & LEMON CURD RIPPLE, STRAWBERRIES

Here, I'm living and loving the flavours of the Amalfi coast through one of the best cheat cakes ever. It's an absolute delight to build and eat, and makes a really special centrepiece, with minimal effort.

SERVES 8 TO 10 | **TOTAL 18 MINUTES**

1 x 750g panettone

2 x 225g fresh strawberries

500g ricotta cheese (cold)

1 tablespoon runny honey

3 heaped tablespoons lemon curd

Unleash the panettone from its packaging and slice off 3 chunky rounds, roughly 2.5cm thick (save the rest of the panettone for lovely breakfasty things). Very finely grate 3 strawberries into a bowl and stir in 1 teaspoon of extra virgin olive oil, then spread this over one side of each of the three rounds and leave to soak in. Whiz the ricotta in a food processor with the honey until silky-smooth, then divide between the rounds and ripple each with lemon curd (give the lemon curd a stir in the jar first, to loosen). Hull and finely slice most of the remaining strawberries (leaving a few pretty ones aside for decorating later), then arrange over two of the layers. Stack up the layers, using a mixture of whole and sliced strawberries to decorate the top. Chill in the fridge until you're ready to serve.

PS

If you feel like you want to do something exciting, pour a quarter of a jar of honey into a pan and place over a medium heat. Leave to bubble away until you have a dark caramel (never touch it!). Allow to cool for 5 minutes, then carefully dip in whole strawberries, holding each above the pan so the caramel drips down, to create wisps of spun sugar. Place upside down on greaseproof (so they don't stick) to set, then use to decorate your cake. To clean the pan effortlessly, pour in 2.5cm of water, pop the lid on and simmer for 5 minutes.

ENERGY	FAT	SAT FAT	PROTEIN	CARBS	SUGARS	SALT	FIBRE
464kcal	18.6g	11.7g	13g	60.6g	32.8g	0.8g	4.3g

AMAZING BAKED APRICOTS
HONEY MERINGUE, FLAKED ALMONDS & DARK CHOCOLATE DRIZZLE

I love celebrating stone fruit, in this case apricots, though peaches, plums or cherries would be just as delicious. With a twisted French-inspired frangipane and meringue, it's the perfect pudding mash-up.

SERVES 8 | **TOTAL 40 MINUTES**

300g flaked almonds

2 x 411g tins of apricot halves in juice

250g runny honey

3 large eggs

50g dark chocolate (70%)

Preheat the oven to 180°C. Place 270g of flaked almonds in a food processor and whiz until super-fine. Drain the apricots, reserving the juices, and put the fruit into a large baking dish. Pour the juices into the food processor, then add 100g of the honey and 3 tablespoons of olive oil. Separate the eggs, adding the yolks to the processor (reserve the whites for later), and whiz until smooth. Evenly pour the mixture over the apricots and bake for 25 minutes.

With 10 minutes to go, whisk the egg whites in a free-standing mixer with a pinch of sea salt until stiff. Heat the remaining honey with 1 tablespoon of water in a small pan over a medium heat until boiling. With the mixer still running at a high speed, slowly, steadily and carefully pour in the boiling honey. Once incorporated, keep whisking for 6 minutes, or until the bowl feels cool. Remove the baking dish from the oven and spoon over the meringue, then scatter over the reserved almonds. Bake for a final 5 minutes while you melt the chocolate over a pan of simmering water, then drizzle it over to finish.

ENERGY	FAT	SAT FAT	PROTEIN	CARBS	SUGARS	SALT	FIBRE
440kcal	29.5g	3.8g	11.2g	34.5g	33.4g	0.3g	0.5g

BREAKFAST BREAD
BOMBS OF FRUITY JAM & HUNG YOGHURT

Prompted by the delicious sweet breads I devoured in Marseille, this recipe makes a fine breakfast or brunch. It's not traditionally French, but that's Marseille – a melting pot of beautiful cultures.

SERVES 10 | **TOTAL 2 HOURS 45 MINUTES**

1 x 7g sachet of dried yeast

500g natural yoghurt

50g unsalted butter (softened)

500g strong bread flour

½ x 370g jar of your favourite fruit jam

In a jug, mix the yeast into 300ml of lukewarm water. Add 50g of the yoghurt, roughly chop and add half the butter, then stir together and leave for a few minutes. Put the flour and 1 teaspoon of sea salt into a large bowl and make a well in the middle. Now gradually pour the yeast mixture into the well, stirring and bringing in the flour from the outside with a fork to form a dough. Knead on a flour-dusted surface for 10 minutes, or until smooth and springy. Cover with a clean damp tea towel and prove in a warm place for 1 hour, or until doubled in size. Meanwhile, line a sieve with pieces of kitchen paper, tip in the remaining yoghurt, then pull up the paper and very gently apply pressure so that the liquid starts to drip through into a bowl. Leave in the fridge to drain.

Knock the air out of the dough, then place in a lightly oiled 30cm non-stick ovenproof frying pan and stretch to fit the pan. With flour-dusted hands, poke your fingers deep into the dough to make lots of little wells, then spoon in small blobs of jam and leave to prove for 1 further hour. Preheat the oven to 180°C and bake for 25 minutes, or until golden and cooked through. Carefully rub over the remaining butter and allow to melt, then move to a board ready to slice. Serve with the hung yoghurt.

ENERGY	FAT	SAT FAT	PROTEIN	CARBS	SUGARS	SALT	FIBRE
293kcal	6.9g	4.1g	8.4g	51.6g	12.5g	0.5g	1.9g

POSH LOLLIPOPS
RICE PUD, STRAWBERRY, ROSE WATER, CHOC & SPRINKLES

When I was researching in Tunisia, it was outrageously hot, and this recipe is inspired by some of the street vendors who were really embellishing the concept of a lollipop – here's my fruity version.

SERVES 6 TO 8 (DEPENDING ON YOUR MOULDS) | **TOTAL 15 MINUTES, PLUS FREEZING**

1 x 400g tin of rice pudding

300g very ripe strawberries

½ teaspoon rose water

100g milk chocolate

1 tablespoon of your favourite sprinkles, such as hundreds and thousands or bashed pistachios

Tip the rice pudding into a blender and whiz until super-smooth. Pour half into a bowl, then divide the rest between your chosen lolly moulds and freeze. Hull the strawberries, then blitz in the blender (give it a quick rinse first) with the rose water until smooth. Stir half into the rest of the rice pudding, then, once the first layer is firm, gently pour into the moulds. Poke in the lollipop sticks and freeze again. Once the second layer is firm, pour in the rest of the strawberry mixture and freeze overnight. To serve, remove from the freezer and gently ease from the moulds. Gently melt the chocolate, then dunk the lollipops in or drizzle with the melted chocolate and finish with your favourite sprinkles.

ENERGY	FAT	SAT FAT	PROTEIN	CARBS	SUGARS	SALT	FIBRE
186kcal	6.5g	3.8g	4.3g	29.1g	22.3g	0.1g	2.3g

BAKED CHEESECAKE
CREAM CHEESE & VANILLA BEAN PASTE

Inspired by the much-loved baked cheesecakes you find in parts of the Mediterranean, this tasty, cheeky little pudding is dead easy to put together, but the finished result looks super-impressive.

SERVES 12 | **PREP 10 MINUTES** | **COOK 24 MINUTES, PLUS CHILLING**

300g icing sugar, plus extra for dusting

4 x 280g tubs of cream cheese

5 teaspoons vanilla bean paste

5 large eggs

70g plain flour

Preheat the oven to 220°C. Boil the kettle. Line the base of a 23cm springform cake tin with a round of greaseproof paper, rub the tin with a little olive oil and lightly dust with icing sugar. Sieve 300g of icing sugar into a large bowl and beat with the cream cheese and vanilla until smooth, then – one at a time – whisk in the eggs, and finally sieve and whisk in the flour. Pour into the lined tin, wrap the base in tin foil to protect the seal, then place inside a deep roasting tray and carefully half-fill the tray with boiling kettle water. Bake on the top shelf of the oven for 20 minutes, or until golden and loosely set in the middle, with a slight wobble. Leave to cool in the water for 15 minutes, then put aside to cool completely. Cover, then chill for at least 4 hours before slicing. Delicious with fresh seasonal fruit.

ENERGY	FAT	SAT FAT	PROTEIN	CARBS	SUGARS	SALT	FIBRE
419kcal	28.3g	18.5g	7.9g	24.6g	29g	0.6g	1.6g

EASY PEACH GRANITA
SWEET VANILLA, FRESH MINT, YOGHURT & VODKA

This is one of the easiest, most refreshing puds, and minus the booze it's super-healthy. Have a play around with plums, strawberries, raspberries or melon, or experiment with your favourite combos.

SERVES 6 | **TOTAL 6 MINUTES, PLUS FREEZING**

2 ripe peaches or 1 x 410g tin of sliced peaches in juice

3 sprigs of fresh mint

2 teaspoons vanilla paste, plus extra to serve

500g Greek yoghurt

150ml vodka or grappa

Slice up the peaches (peel and destone if using fresh and drain if using tinned), lay flat inside a reusable bag and freeze overnight. When you're ready to serve, break the peaches into a food processor and whiz with a couple of mint leaves and the vanilla bean paste. To serve, divide the yoghurt between six chilled serving bowls, spoon over the granita, pick over the remaining mint leaves and drizzle with a little more vanilla bean paste. Serve with a shot of chilled booze and some extra peach, if you like.

ENERGY	FAT	SAT FAT	PROTEIN	CARBS	SUGARS	SALT	FIBRE
187kcal	8g	4.9g	4.4g	10.9g	10.8g	0.2g	0.8g

SMASHIN' SEMIFREDDO
CHOCOLATE HONEYCOMB, CHERRIES & HAZELNUTS

Outrageously delicious, this is a brilliant pud to try at home and is far more manageable than making ice cream – you can make it weeks in advance, and also play around with your flavour combos.

SERVES 12 | **TOTAL 15 MINUTES, PLUS FREEZING**

5 x 40g Crunchie bars (chilled)

200g glacé Morello cherries

100g blanched hazelnuts

4 large eggs

600ml double cream

Place a 30cm serving dish in the freezer. Smash the Crunchie bars to a dust, and finely chop the cherries. Toast the hazelnuts in a dry frying pan until golden all over, then finely chop or smash them. Separate the eggs, putting the whites into one bowl and the yolks into another. With a super-clean whisk, whip the whites with a pinch of sea salt until very stiff. In a separate bowl, whisk the cream until it forms silky, delicate soft peaks (which means thickened, but don't over-whip it). Whisk up the yolks, then gently fold into the whites, followed by the cream, keeping in as much air as possible. Fold through the smashed Crunchie bars, cherries and hazelnuts, then transfer to the frozen serving dish, cover and freeze for at least 4 hours, or until set (it'll keep for 2 weeks in the freezer).

Around 2 hours before you want to enjoy your dessert, remove it from the freezer to the fridge and gently thaw it until 'semi-freddo' or semi-frozen – you're looking for a texture similar to ice cream. When you serve it, it's nice to sprinkle the top with some of the same ingredients, to decorate.

ENERGY	FAT	SAT FAT	PROTEIN	CARBS	SUGARS	SALT	FIBRE
435kcal	35.5g	18.4g	4.9g	24.6g	22.9g	0.3g	0.9g

HELPFUL KITCHEN NOTES

CELEBRATE QUALITY & SEASONALITY

As is often the case in cooking, using quality ingredients really does make a difference to the success of the recipes. There's not loads of stuff to buy for each recipe, so I'm hoping that will give you the excuse to trade up where you can, buying the best veggies, fish or meat you can find. Also, remember that shopping in season always allows your food to be more delicious and affordable. When it comes to veg and fruit, remember to give everything a nice wash before you start cooking, especially if you're using stuff raw.

Ingredients that noticeably make a difference on the flavour front when you choose best quality are: chorizo, sausages, black pudding, cheese, jarred beans and chickpeas, tinned plum tomatoes, Maldon sea salt and dark chocolate.

FOCUSING ON FISH & SEAFOOD

Fish and seafood are an incredibly delicious source of protein, but literally the minute they're caught they start to deteriorate in freshness, so you want to buy them as close to the day of your meal as you can – I wouldn't endorse them being stored in the fridge for days, you're better off with frozen if that's the case. I recommend planning your fish and seafood dinners around your shopping days.

Make sure you choose responsibly sourced fish and seafood – look for the MSC logo, or talk to your fishmonger and take their advice. Try to mix up your choices, choosing seasonal, sustainable options as they're available. If you can only find farmed fish, make sure you look for the RSPCA Assured or ASC logo to ensure your fish is responsibly sourced.

MEAT & EGGS

When it comes to meat, of course I'm going to endorse higher-welfare farming practices, like organic or free-range. Animals should be raised well, free to roam, display natural behaviours and live a stress-free healthy life. With everything in life, you pay more for quality, and I'm always a believer that if you take a couple of minutes to plan your weekly menus you can be clever about using cheaper cuts of meat, or you could try cooking some of my meat-reduced dishes and vegetarian dishes, which should give you the opportunity to trade up to quality proteins when you do choose them. A few of the cuts of meat in this book require you to go to a butcher, and I cannot recommend this enough – they can be so helpful, they can order stuff in especially for you and can ensure you have the exact weights you need.

When it comes to eggs and anything containing egg, such as pasta or mayonnaise – always choose free-range or organic.

DIAL UP YOUR DAIRY

With staple dairy products, like milk, yoghurt and butter, please trade up to organic if you can. Unlike meat, it is only slightly more expensive and I couldn't recommend it enough, if it's available to you. Every time you buy organic, you vote for a better food system that supports the highest standards of animal welfare, where both cows and land are well looked after.

FRIDGE ORGANIZATION

When juggling space in the fridge, remember that raw meat and fish should be well wrapped and placed on the bottom shelf to avoid cross-contamination. Any food that is ready to eat, whether it's cooked or it doesn't need to be cooked, should be stored on a higher shelf.

THE FREEZER IS YOUR BEST FRIEND

For busy people, without doubt your freezer, if stocked correctly, is your closest ally. There are just a few basic rules when it comes to really utilizing it well. If you're batch cooking, remember to let food cool thoroughly before freezing – break it down into portions so it cools quicker, and get it into the freezer within 2 hours. Make sure everything is well wrapped, and labelled for future reference. Thaw in the fridge before use, and use within 48 hours. If you've frozen cooked food, don't freeze it again after reheating or defrosting it.

Nutritionally speaking, freezing veg and fruit quickly after harvesting retains the nutritional value very efficiently, often trumping fresh equivalents that have been stuck in the supply chain for a while. In this book you will see me using frozen veg (which I love!) and also bags of pre-prepped mixed veg, which give you more variety with just one product, and are super-convenient and widely available. These are fantastic time savers for busy people and I feel it is my duty to shine a light on these handy ingredient hacks, as I know that time is precious.

MAXIMIZING FLAVOUR

In this book I use a lot of what I like to call 'flavour bombs', which are readily available in most supermarkets – they're a super-efficient way to add big bonus flavour, fast. Things like fragrant spice mixes and pastes – ras el hanout, mixed spice, baharat spice mix, harissa and shawarma paste, to name a few – really bolster the flavour of a dish in just one supercharged ingredient. Tahini, pesto, tzatziki and olive tapenade, as well as mixed bags of nuts, dried fruit and seeds, marinated olives (make sure you embrace the marinating ingredients, too!),

and cracking condiments, such as mustard and chilli sauces, will also work hard for you on the flavour front. These items guarantee flavour and consistency, educate your palette and save hours of time in preparation. Most are non-perishable, which means you're not under pressure to use them up super-quickly.

BIGGING UP FRESH HERBS

Fresh herbs are a gift to any cook. Instead of buying them, why not grow them yourself in the garden or in a pot on your windowsill? Herbs allow you to add single-minded flavour to a dish, without the need to over-season, which is good for everyone. They're also packed with all sorts of incredible qualities on the nutritional front – we like that. And don't forget dried herbs – they're not a compromise to fresh, they're just different. Wonderfully, they still retain a huge amount of nutritional value, but it's the dramatic change in flavour that is useful to us cooks. Plus, they're non-perishable and super-convenient to have ready and raring to go. The ones I always have in my pantry are: oregano, dill, mint and thyme, to name just a few.

LET'S CHAT EQUIPMENT

I've kept the equipment I've used in this book pretty simple – a set of saucepans, non-stick ovenproof frying pans and casserole pans, a griddle, some sturdy roasting trays and a couple of baking trays. Of course, a chopping board and a decent set of knives is a given for nearly every recipe, too. If you want to save time, there are a few kitchen gadgets that will make your life a lot easier – things like a speed-peeler, a box grater and a pestle and mortar are all fantastic for creating great texture, and a blender and food processor is always a bonus, especially if you're short on time!

OVEN LOVIN'

All recipes are tested in fan ovens – find conversions for conventional ovens, °F and gas online.

A NOTE FROM JAMIE'S NUTRITION TEAM

Our job is to make sure that Jamie can be super-creative, while also ensuring that all recipes meet our guidelines. Every book has a different brief, and *5 Ingredients Mediterranean* is about arming you with inspiration for every day of the week. With the exception of the Sweet Things chapter, 70% of the recipes fit into our everyday food guidelines, but they're not complete meals, so you'll need to balance out your mealtimes with what's lacking. For clarity and so that you can make informed choices, we've presented easy-to-read nutrition info for each dish on the recipe page (displayed per serving). We also want to inspire a more sustainable way of eating, so 65% of the recipes are either meat-free or meat-reduced (meaning they contain at least 30% less meat than a regular portion size).

Food is fun, joyful and creative – it gives us energy and plays a crucial role in keeping our bodies healthy. Remember, a nutritious, varied and balanced diet and regular exercise are the keys to a healthier lifestyle. We don't label foods as 'good' or 'bad' – there's a place for everything, however you can have a diet that doesn't support good health if the balance isn't quite right. We encourage an understanding of the difference between nutritious foods for everyday consumption and those to be enjoyed occasionally. For more info about our guidelines and how we analyse recipes, please visit jamieoliver.com/nutrition.

Rozzie Batchelar – Senior Nutritionist, RNutr (food)

A BIT ABOUT BALANCE

Balance is key when it comes to eating well. Balance your plate right and keep your portion control in check, and you can be confident that you're giving yourself a great start on the path to good health. It's important to consume a variety of foods to ensure we get the nutrients our bodies need to stay healthy. You don't have to be spot-on every day – just try to get your balance right across the week. If you eat meat and fish, as a general guide for main meals you want at least two portions of fish a week, one of which should be oily. Split the rest of the week's main meals between brilliant plant-based meals, some poultry and a little red meat. An all-vegetarian diet can be perfectly healthy, too.

WHAT'S THE BALANCE

The UK government's Eatwell Guide shows us what a healthy balance of food looks like. The figures below indicate the proportion of each food group that's recommended across the day.

THE FIVE FOOD GROUPS (UK)	PROPORTION
Vegetables and fruit	40%
Starchy carbohydrates (bread, rice, potatoes, pasta)	38%
Protein (lean meat, fish, eggs, beans, other non-dairy sources)	12%
Dairy foods, milk & dairy alternatives	8%
Unsaturated fats (such as oils)	1%
AND DON'T FORGET TO DRINK PLENTY OF WATER, TOO	

Try to only consume foods and drinks high in fat, salt or sugar occasionally.

VEGETABLES & FRUIT

To live a good, healthy life, vegetables and fruit should sit right at the heart of your diet. Veg and fruit come in all kinds of colours, shapes, sizes, flavours and textures, and contain different vitamins and minerals, which each play a part in keeping our bodies healthy and optimal, so variety is key. Eat the rainbow, mixing up your choices as much as you can and embracing the seasons so you're getting produce at its best and its most nutritious. As an absolute minimum, aim for at least 5 portions of fresh, frozen or tinned veg and fruit every day of the week, enjoying more wherever possible. 80g (or a large handful) counts as one portion. You can also count one 30g portion of dried fruit, one 80g portion of beans or pulses, and 150ml of unsweetened veg or fruit juice per day.

STARCHY CARBOHYDRATES

Carbs provide us with a large proportion of the energy needed to make our bodies move, and to ensure our organs have the fuel they need to function. When you can, choose fibre-rich wholegrain and wholewheat varieties. 260g is the recommended daily amount of carbohydrates for the average adult, with up to 90g coming from total sugars, which includes natural sugars found in whole fruit, milk and milk products, and no more than 30g of free sugars. Free sugars are those added to food and drink, including sugar found in honey, syrups, fruit juice and smoothies. Fibre is classified as a carbohydrate and is mainly found in plant-based foods such as wholegrain carbohydrates, veg and fruit. It helps to keep our digestive systems healthy, control our blood-sugar levels and maintain healthy cholesterol levels. Adults should be aiming for at least 30g each day.

PROTEIN

Think of protein as the building blocks of our bodies – it's used for everything that's important to how we grow and repair. Try to vary your proteins to include more beans and pulses, two sources of sustainably sourced fish per week (one of which is oily), and reduce red and processed meat if your diet is high in these. Choose lean cuts of animal-based protein where you can. Beans, peas and lentils are great alternatives to meat because they're naturally low in fat and, as well as protein, they contain fibre and some vitamins and minerals. Other nutritious protein sources include tofu, eggs, nuts and seeds. Variety is key! The requirement for an average woman aged 19 to 50 is 45g per day, with 55g for men in the same age bracket.

DAIRY FOODS, MILK & DAIRY ALTERNATIVES

This food group offers an amazing array of nutrients when eaten in the right amounts. Favour organic dairy milk and yoghurt, and small amounts of cheese in this category; the lower-fat varieties (with no added sugar) are equally brilliant and worth embracing. If opting for plant-based versions, I think it's great that we have choice, but it's really important to look for unsweetened fortified options that have added calcium, iodine and vitamin B12 in the ingredients list, to avoid missing out on the key nutrients provided by dairy milk.

UNSATURATED FATS

While we only need small amounts, we do require healthier fats. Choose unsaturated sources where you can, such as olive and liquid vegetable oils, nuts, seeds, avocado and omega-3 rich oily fish. Generally speaking, it's recommended that the average woman has no more than 70g of fat per day, with less than 20g of that from saturated fat, and the average man no more than 90g, with less than 30g from saturated fat.

DRINK PLENTY OF WATER

To be the best you can be, stay hydrated. Water is essential to life, and to every function of the human body! In general, women aged 14 and over need at least 2 litres per day and men in the same age bracket need at least 2.5 litres per day.

ENERGY & NUTRITION INFO

The average woman needs 2,000 calories a day, while the average man needs roughly 2,500. These figures are a rough guide, and what we eat needs to be considered in relation to factors like age, build, lifestyle and activity levels.

WITH LOVE & THANKS

Rest assured, even though this is book number 27 (can you believe it?), it doesn't make my gratitude any less than on book one. Over the years, my obsession and dedication to writing the very best cookbook I possibly can has never faltered, and backed up and supported by my incredible team, many of whom have been with me since the very beginning, we've done some truly brilliant work that I am – and you should be – massively proud of.

First up, huge thanks to my super-talented in-house food team. To the wonderful Ginny Rolfe, who's been with me for the whole ride – writing a book without her by my side just wouldn't be the same. To the fantastic Maddie Rix, Rachel Young, Ruth Tebby, Sharon Sharpe, Becky Merrick and Helen Martin. To my trusty sidekicks Pete Begg and Bobby Sebire. And to our extended food team family, Jodene Jordan, Hugo Harrison, Isla Murray, Sophie Mackinnon, Johnny Guselli and George Stocks. You guys are all a joy to work with.

Big shout-out to the wonderful Rozzie Batchelar on nutrition, and the illustrious Lucinda Cobb on technical. Thanks for keeping me in check.

On words, thanks to the lovely Beth Stroud for taking the reins, to the master of testing Jade Melling, and to Sumaya Steele and the rest of the editorial team. Special mention to my Editor-in-Chief, Rebecca Verity, who's off on maternity leave but always watching from afar, and to her cover, Rebecca Morten.

Huge thanks to Creative Director James Verity on design – amazing job, as always. And shout out to Devon Jeffs and the rest of the team, too.

Big love to David Loftus, our long-serving photography don – thank you as ever, and thanks also to Richard Bowyer for assisting. Shout out to Chris Terry for the lovely portraits and travel pics, and to Konstantinos Sofikitis, Samy Frihka and Edwidge Lamy for the beautiful reportage photography.

Massive thanks to my ever-supportive family at Penguin Random House – what a hard-working bunch you are! To Tom Weldon, Louise Moore, Elizabeth Smith, Clare Parker, Tom Troughton, Ella Watkins, Kallie Townsend, Juliette Butler, Katherine Tibbals, Lee Motley, Sarah Fraser, Nick Lowndes, Christina Ellicott, Sophie Marston, Laura Garrod, Kelly Mason, Emma Carter, Hannah Padgham, Chris Wyatt, Tracy Orchard, Chantal Noel, Catherine Wood, Anjali Nathani, Kate Reiners, Tyra Burr, Joanna Whitehead, Madeleine Stephenson, Lee-Anne Williams, Jessica Meredeen, Sarah Porter, Grace Dellar, Stuart Anderson, Anna Curvis, Akua Akowuah, Samantha Waide and Carrie Anderson. Also to Annie Lee, Jill Cole, Emma Horton and Ruth Ellis.

Lots of love to my team back at JO HQ – you are all amazing. Special mention goes to those closest to the production and promotion of this book – to my marketing maestros Rosalind Godber and Michelle Dam, and Tamsyn Zeitsman on PR. To Bryony Palmer and the rest of the social team, to Rich Herd and the VPU team, and to the steadfast finance team, especially Pamela Lovelock, the lovely Therese MacDermott and John Dewar, who work tirelessly in the background. Big love to Giovanna Milia and the legal team, and to the personnel, operations, IT, P&D and facilities teams. Thanks for all your hard work and dedication, as always. And props to my keen team of office testers – thanks for your diligence.

I must thank my CEO Kevin Styles, Deputy Louise Holland, Media MD and stalwart Zoe Collins, and my thoughtful EA Ali Solway.

Thanks also to Izzeldin A. Bukhari and Georgina Hayden for the foodie chats and inspiration. And to the talented potters at Alanda Wilson Ceramics and Sytch Farm studios – I love to find and collect new plates and crockery, and yours are just beautiful.

On the TV side of things, thanks for all your hard work and wonderful memories. To Sean Moxhay, Sam Beddoes, Katie Millard, Jamie Hammick, Sarah Durdin Roberston, Ben Prager, Renzo Luzardo, Tanya Cook and Mee-ling Ho. I would also like to acknowledge the wonderful local fixer teams in each of our locations. To Tobie Tripp for the music, and to the team over at Channel 4, and Fremantle, too.

And of course – to my beautiful family for your constant support.

LOVE YOU ALL X

INDEX

Recipes marked V are suitable for vegetarians; in some instances you'll need to swap in a vegetarian alternative to cheese such as Parmesan.

For a quick reference list of all the vegetarian, vegan, dairy-free and gluten-free recipes in this book, visit:

jamieoliver.com/5ingredientsmed/reference

THE JAMIE OLIVER COLLECTION

HUNGRY FOR MORE?

For handy nutrition advice, as well as videos, features, hints, tricks and tips on all sorts of different subjects, loads of brilliant recipes, plus much more, check out

JAMIEOLIVER.COM   #5INGREDIENTSMED

PENGUIN MICHAEL JOSEPH

UK | USA | CANADA | IRELAND | AUSTRALIA | INDIA | NEW ZEALAND | SOUTH AFRICA

Penguin Michael Joseph is part of the Penguin Random House group of companies, whose addresses can be found at global.penguinrandomhouse.com

Penguin
Random House
UK

First published 2023

001

Copyright © Jamie Oliver, 2023

Recipe photography copyright © Jamie Oliver Enterprises Limited, 2023

Portrait photography copyright © Chris Terry, 2023

© 2007 P22 Underground Pro Demi. All Rights Reserved, P22 Type Foundry, Inc.

The moral right of the author has been asserted

Cover & recipe photography by David Loftus

Portrait photography by Chris Terry: pp. 2, 6–7, 12, 174–5, 320, back cover

Travel photography by Chris Terry, Jamie Oliver, Konstantinos Sofikitis, Samy Frikha & Edwidge Lamy: pp. 10–11, 70–71, 150–51, 230–31

Design by Jamie Oliver Limited

Colour reproduction by Altaimage Ltd

Printed in Germany by Mohn Media

The authorized representative in the EEA is Penguin Random House Ireland, Morrison Chambers, 32 Nassau Street, Dublin D02 YH68

A CIP catalogue record for this book is available from the British Library

ISBN: 978–0–241–43116–0

penguin.co.uk

jamieoliver.com

www.greenpenguin.co.uk